# Will the Revolution be Televised?
# A Marxist Analysis of the Media

John Molyneux

GW00393155

*Bookmarks Publications*

**Will the Revolution be Televised? A Marxist Analysis of the Media**
John Molyneux

First published in 2011 by Bookmarks Publications
c/o 1 Bloomsbury Street, London WC1B 3QE
© Bookmarks Publications

Typeset by Phil Whaite
Printed by Russell Press

ISBN 9781905192915

# Contents

## About the author

John Molyneux is a socialist writer and activist, formerly a lecturer at Portsmouth University and now living in Dublin. His publications include *Marxism and the Party* (1978), *What is the Real Marxist Tradition?* (1985) and *Rembrandt and Revolution* (2001). He is a member of the Socialist Workers Party in Britain and Ireland.

# Preface

As this small book was nearing completion two events occurred which had significant bearing on its subject matter, namely the Murdoch phone hacking scandal and the August 2011 riots.

What the Murdoch scandal demonstrated was: first, the shameless amorality of the *News of the World* and the rest of the News Corp operation; second, the close collaboration between nominally independent institutions (politicians, government, police, press, etc) which constitute different wings of the ruling class; third, that when push came to shove Murdoch and co were not as all-powerful as some people imagined. It thus reinforced a number of my main arguments and I have incorporated some comments on this scandal within the text. I have also included as an Appendix an article on the scandal I wrote for *Socialist Worker* in Ireland.

The media coverage of the riots, which exploded in Tottenham on Saturday 6 August and then spread rapidly to other parts of London and then other British cities, proved to be a classic example of well-established patterns of reporting. In chapter 1, I discuss reporting of demonstrations and note how the media has long operated "a very neat trick worthy of *Catch-22*. If the demonstration passes off peacefully, even if it is very large, it is often given almost no coverage at all... If on the other hand there is some kind of trouble or 'violence' the media will give the demo massive coverage but will focus entirely on condemning the demonstrators." I then note that:

Similar media "storms" have been whipped up against demonstrators on many occasions since then including the SWP anti-fascists who broke up the National Front march in Lewisham in 1977, the miners' mass picket at Orgreave in 1984, the Poll Tax Riot of 1990, the Anti Nazi League confrontation with police when trying to march to BNP headquarters in Welling in 1999 and, of course, the recent student demos in November/December 2010. Moreover these storms invariably result in the identification and prosecution of individual protesters as well as preparing the ground for "exemplary" sentences.

The media storm in response to the riots was of exceptional intensity and close to unanimous. The *Guardian* has posted online the front pages of the main papers for Tuesday 9 August.[1] Here are some examples:

*Daily Express*: "Flaming Morons—thugs and thieves terrorise Britain's streets"
*Daily Mail*: "The Anarchy Spreads" plus comment in box: "To blame the cuts is immoral and cynical. This is criminality pure and simple."
*Daily Telegraph*: "Rule of the Mob"
*Independent*: "Mob Rule"
*Daily Star*: "Anarchy in the UK"
*Daily Mirror*: "Yob Rule"
*Metro*: "Riots: The Madness Spreads"

The only exceptions to this unanimity were the *Guardian* with the relatively neutral "The Battle for London" and the *Financial Times* which had its own priorities: "Stocks Plummet on US Downgrade". Interestingly, the *Express*, *Mail* and *Star* all used the same photograph of a masked rioter in front of a blazing car, the *Independent* and the *Metro* used a very similar photograph of a different rioter in front of a burning car, and the *Telegraph*, the *Guardian* and the *Mirror* used the same photo of a woman jumping from a burning building. In other words the papers, almost with one voice, echoed and reinforced the government/police/establishment line of condemning and denouncing the rioters.

Central to this denunciation was the insistence, led by David Cameron, that the rioting was "pure criminality", ie the riots had no political motive or political or social context. Cameron as prime minister, and therefore supposed to be in charge of the social and political context, had an obvious vested interest in claiming that this was irrelevant, and the media not only agreed with this implausible claim but tried to create a climate of hostility to anyone who argued otherwise. The BBC News Channel showed an interview with veteran black activist and broadcaster Darcus Howe, in which he called the riots "an insurrection" and spoke about police racism and harassment of young blacks. The interviewer, Fiona Armstrong, knowing that this was not the sort of thing that should be being said, immediately went on to the attack and suggested that Howe, himself, had been a rioter in the past.[2] Later the BBC apologised for Armstrong's remarks, but the point is if she made an error it was an error in doing what she knew was required of her, namely to stigmatise and marginalise anyone challenging the consensus.

Again this episode reinforced a general point made in the text:

> The [pro-capitalist] bias also affects how interviews are conducted. A quite different tone and manner is adopted when the interviewee is a "respected" mainstream politician from when he/she is the representative of some "extremist" or "disapproved of", ie anti-capitalist, cause...
>
> Media people—successful journalists, editors, presenters, producers etc, get where they are partly through their ability to keep their finger on the pulse, to sense the mood, not so much among the general public, certainly not in the working class, but among the middle class and above all the establishment.

As for my statement that these "media storms" invariably prepare the way "for exemplary sentences", the response to the riots has confirmed it with it a vengeance. Innumerable opinion pieces have been published applauding "the admirably tough sentences courts have dished out to looters" (the *Sun*[3]); hoping that "the police round up these electronic ringleaders and charge them with incitement" (Richard Littlejohn[4]); complaining of "the hand-wringers of Britain's left-liberal establishment"[5] and decrying any attempt at understanding, like Tony Parsons in the *Daily Mirror*:

> Trying to understand the feelings of the rioters is like trying to understand the feelings of a man who has boot pressed against your throat... Frankly, my dear, many of us do not have the stomach for sympathy right now. We just want to see the rioters banged up and stewing in their own filth... Why did the riots happen? Because we live with a lot of scum in our midst.[6]

It is very tempting to dismiss this kind of journalism as "mindless thuggery" but one of the tasks attempted in this booklet is to uncover the cause of such coverage and show whose interests it serves.

In undertaking this task I, like anyone else making a radical critique of the media, owe a particular debt which I should acknowledge here, to two pioneering bodies of work. First, that of the Glasgow University Media Group (Greg Philo et al) who in a stream of books, beginning with *Bad News* in 1976, have offered forensic dissections of British television news coverage, demonstrating beyond reasonable doubt its systematic bias in favour of those who run our society. Second, that of Noam Chomsky, who (with Edward S Herman) in *Manufacturing Consent* (1988), and in *Necessary Illusions* (1989) and in numerous articles has performed the same operation in relation to the US media. If I differ somewhat from these authors in my conclusions, especially as regards what needs to be done about the problem, this does not diminish the usefulness of their analyses. I have also found particularly useful two articles by Colin Sparks, "Inside the Media" in *International Socialism* 98 (spring 2003) and "Reality TV: the Big Brother Phenomenon" in *International Socialism* 114 (spring 2007).

Finally, and I hope appropriately, I would like to dedicate this work to the memory of the late Paul Foot, one of the outstanding radical journalists of our time.

**John Molyneux**
21 August 2011

# Introduction

Many of the bare facts about the world we live in are truly shocking. For example, the fact that that the 358 richest people in the world have as much personal wealth as the entire lower half of the world's population, about 3,000 million people. Or the fact that in 2010 world armaments spending stood at $1,660 billion, nearly half of which ($696 billion) was accounted for by the US alone, while the number of people suffering from acute poverty and malnutrition was, according to the UN, about 1,000 million. In other words, the US, where people tend to overeat, spends over $696 per starving person in the world on weapons designed to kill people, and which are actually capable of killing every person in the world several times over. The Stockholm International Peace Research Institute (SIPRI) reports as follows:

> World military spending increased by 5.9 percent to hit a new record high of $1.53 trillion in 2009... The rise in military spending was achieved in the face of the ongoing international economic downturn.
>
> Worldwide military spending has grown by 49 percent since 2000... The far-reaching effects of the global financial crisis and economic recession appear to have had little impact on world military expenditure.[7]

At the same time in country after country—the US, Britain, France, Greece, Spain, Portugal and Ireland are obvious examples—pensioners, students, the unemployed, public sector workers and other ordinary people are being presented with the bill to pay for the bailout of the banking system.

And yet most of the time most people more or less accept this state of affairs. They may not like it but they are sufficiently reconciled to it for it to able to continue. Why? Part of the answer—though by no means the whole answer—is the media.

For all of the facts cited above there are widely circulated justifications. Inequality is justified because without incentives people won't work hard and because wealth is a reward for hard work or intelligence or entrepreneurial genius. Besides which they, the rich, provide work for the rest of us and without them we would all be unemployed. As for the huge sums spent on arms, they are justified in each country by the huge sums being spent in every other country, ie it is claimed they are necessary for defence; indeed that's what these expenditures are called: defence spending. The exceptionally huge spending of the US is justified because it is the best country in the world and because it has to defend not only itself but all the free world; indeed the United States armed forces are the principal defence of the cause of freedom as such.

These arguments are so widely circulated that to many people they seem almost like facts or "common sense". One of the main reasons for this is that they receive a huge amount of media airtime and column inches. These arguments are also circulated by word of mouth, of course—by parents, friends, teachers, lecturers, in pubs and clubs, and so on—partly because people receive them so frequently from the media. Conversely there are well-established replies to the justifications of inequality and arms spending, for example that arms spending is not primarily for defence of freedom at all, but to defend the wealth and power, domestically and internationally, of the rich. But one has only to state that view to realise that it sounds different from the first set of arguments: instead of sounding like common sense it sounds slightly strange, outlandish even, maybe one of those "conspiracy theories". And one of the main reasons for this is that such views are much less featured in the media and when they do appear are always presented as highly contentious.

In *Nineteen Eighty-Four* George Orwell describes the moment when the society, Oceania, switches from being at war with Eurasia to being at war with Eastasia:

> Winston was taking part in a demonstration in one of the central London squares at the moment when it happened... On a scarlet-draped platform an orator of the Inner Party... was haranguing the crowd... His voice, made metallic by the amplifiers, boomed forth an endless catalogue of atrocities, massacres, deportations, lootings, rapings, torture of prisoners, bombing of civilians, lying propaganda, unjust aggressions, broken treaties. It was almost impossible to listen to him without being first convinced and then maddened... The speech had been proceeding for perhaps 20 minutes when a messenger hurried on to the platform and a scrap of paper was slipped into the speaker's hand. He unrolled and read it without pausing in his speech. Nothing altered in his voice or manner, or in the content of what he was saying, but suddenly the names were different. Without words said, a wave of understanding rippled through the crowd. Oceania was at war with Eastasia! The next moment there was a tremendous commotion. The banners and posters with which the square was decorated were all wrong... There was a riotous interlude while posters were ripped from the walls, banners torn to shreds and trampled underfoot... But within two or three minutes it was all over. The orator, still gripping the neck of the microphone, his shoulders hunched forward, his free hand clawing at the air, had gone straight on with his speech. One minute more, and the feral roars of rage were again bursting from the crowd. The Hate continued exactly as before, except that the target had been changed.[8]

Moreover, from that moment it was claimed and believed that Oceania had always been at war with Eastasia and Eurasia had always been an ally.

Sometimes it seems as though, with only a little exaggeration, our society works like this. For about 45 years, from the Second World War to the fall of the Berlin Wall, the enemy of "the West" (the US and its allies) was Communism (the Soviet Union and its allies, and all those who sympathised with its ideology). Communism was seen as aggressive, bent on world domination, inherently tyrannical, and the main force for evil in the world. In the name of combating Communism it was considered reasonable to construct the most powerful arsenal of weapons of mass destruction the world has ever seen, and lay down plans for the use of these weapons on the cities of the Soviet Union (and other "communist" centres) with the certainty of killing tens of millions of civilians; to wage several major hot wars (notably the Korean War with approximately three million casualties and the Vietnam War with a similar death toll); to invade numerous countries (Cuba, Guatemala, Grenada, etc); to wage proxy wars in a number of others (El Salvador, Nicaragua); to support a range of dictators and torturers (Somoza in Nicaragua, Pinochet in Chile, Sukarno and Suharto in Indonesia, Marcos in the Philippines, Saddam Hussein in Iraq, South African apartheid etc) and various Islamist forces such as the rulers of Saudi Arabia, and the Taliban in Afghanistan (against the Soviet invasion).

Then, more or less as Communism collapsed, a switch was thrown, and the enemy of the West became "Islamic fundamentalism" and terrorism. As with Communism before it, this enemy is aggressive, bent on world domination, and evil. In the name of combating this enemy it has been necessary to wage two major wars (Afghanistan and Iraq) and various proxy wars (particularly in the horn of Africa); support Israel whatever it does; support various dictators and torturers, including Muslim dictators and torturers (such as the Saudis, again, and Mubarak of Egypt); establish the torture camps at Guantanamo and Abu Ghraib, practise extraordinary rendition, and endorse water-boarding. At the same time the conflict between the West and Islam has been projected all the way back to the Crusades and theorised as a "clash of civilisations"* in which the West represents enlightenment, reason, tolerance and modernity, while Islam embodies backwardness, irrationality, prejudice and violence.

And both these campaigns and the more or less seamless transition between them were aided and abetted by a cooperative media that simply substituted demonising Islam for demonising Communism.

If this comparison is valid, and in some respects it is, the key questions to be answered are: (a) who sends the order to the orator/throws the switch at CNN or Fox News? and (b) why do people slavishly believe and/or do what they are told? This pamphlet will address these questions.

However, it is also clear that whatever the parallels may be between Western society today and Orwell's dystopian vision, there are also significant differences. For example, the media in our society is not simply, or even mainly, government controlled propaganda. Large sections of it regularly attack or criticise the government of the day, and even those sectors of the media that are state owned frequently allow dissident views to be aired. Nor is it actually the case that the vast majority of people always follow the dominant media line. Most obviously, despite strong pro-war media pressure, many millions of people round the world marched and protested against the Iraq war. Of course these mass protests did not succeed in preventing the war but that was because Bush and Blair retained the political and military power to wage

---

\* See Samuel P Huntington, *The Clash of Civilizations and the Remaking of World Order* (New York, 1996).

it, not because they persuaded everybody that it was a good idea. Consequently there are more complex, and to some extent more difficult, issues which also have to be discussed: to what extent is the media biased and what is the precise nature of its bias; why do people choose the media they do; how effective is the media in controlling or influencing what people think and what they do?

Besides flagging up these questions I also want to say something at the outset about my own bias. Many sections of the media, for example the BBC, claim to be politically neutral. For reasons I shall make clear I do not accept this claim; indeed I will argue that it is thoroughly misleading. I do not therefore intend to practise the same deceit myself. This pamphlet is not politically neutral. It is written explicitly from the standpoint of wanting to change the world, and more than that of wanting to change the world in the direction of socialism, by which I mean a society under the democratic control of working people and based on production for human need, not profit. For this reason I shall also be addressing the question of how the influence of the media as presently constituted can be combated and, ultimately, transformed.

It is also written from the standpoint of Marxism and aims to show, in passing as it were, that a Marxist analysis of society is key to the understanding of the media.

# 1. Media bias

As a longstanding activist I have occasionally been interviewed by or appeared on the media, mostly in connection with demonstrations or campaigns. From time to time I have raised with the journalist concerned the issue of media bias. Almost invariably they have completely denied the charge, and insisted that they were only there to report the facts and represent all points of view. I was never quite sure whether they were trained to say this, much as a call centre worker has a script from which they are not allowed to deviate, or actually believed it. Similarly if you watch political discussion programmes such as the BBC's *Question Time* you may have noticed that if any one of the panel or the audience challenges the programme's political neutrality the presenter, David Dimbleby or whoever, immediately leaps to the defence of their employers—abandoning any pretence of their own neutrality—to insist on the absolute fairness and lack of bias of the programme.

However, the fact is that, despite all these denials, the media is profoundly politically, socially, ideologically and culturally biased. This applies not just to some of the media—to the *Daily Mail* but not the *Independent*, to newspapers but not TV, to the US and Britain but not the rest of the world—but to all the media everywhere. And the first thing I want to argue is that this must be so. I am not complaining about it. It cannot be otherwise.

The reason for this is very simple. It is impossible to produce an unbiased news bulletin, newspaper, magazine, radio programme or whatever because every minute of every hour of every day a more or less infinite number of events occur and they cannot all be reported—indeed very few of them can be. Instead there has to a rigorous process of selection which involves judgements as to what is important, "newsworthy", interesting, etc, and those judgements are inherently political and ideological, even if the people making them don't realise it. Indeed the less the people making the judgements (editors, producers, journalists) appreciate this, the more they think their selections are simply "obvious" and "natural", the more biased they are.

Let me give a couple of examples. Each year in the UK approximately 235,000 couples get married—that's about 644 per day. The vast majority of these weddings will get no media coverage at all. However, when a certain William Windsor married Kate Middleton on 29 April 2011 it received blanket media coverage before, during and after the event. This, of course, is because William Windsor is the son of Charles Windsor who is the son of Elizabeth Windsor who is the queen and it is therefore a "Royal Wedding". The disparity between the coverage of a royal and an ordinary wedding reflects and simultaneously reinforces the view, held by virtually all the media and by the government and by the main opposition party (at the moment the Labour Party), and most of the British establishment that more or less anything and everything the royals do is more important and more interesting than the same things done by the rest of us. In other words it reflects the media's commitment, along with that of the state and the establishment, to the institution and ideology of monarchy. It is a political bias.

Another example: as I am writing these lines there is large-scale flooding in Brazil. It is the worst natural disaster in Brazil for decades and more than 500 people have died. On the BBC News website this is the third item on its home page (dealing with world news) below rumours about Silvio Berlusconi and a teenage dancer and just above the pope's plans to beatify Pope John Paul II. The *Guardian* website has much more coverage, the *Sun*, the *Daily Mirror* and the

*Daily Mail* virtually nothing between them. None of this is surprising—again it reflects the values and choices of these different media outlets. If the event had occurred in Britain obviously the coverage would have been massive, but it is also the case that if it had been in the US it would have received enormously more coverage than when it is Brazil. This is because it is generally accepted by most of the British media that what happens in the US is more important and more interesting than what happens anywhere else in the world except in Britain itself.

What both these examples show is that even before we come to the question of how stories are reported a major element of bias enters the media in what is reported at all. And this is unavoidable. Faced with accusations of bias there is one argument that media representatives and apologists often come up with. They say we are being attacked by the right for being biased to the left and by the left for being biased to the right, so that shows we are more or less in the correct unbiased place. This does indeed happen, and I shall say more about this later, but the conclusion does not at all follow. First, it is necessary to understand that the centre, the so-called middle of the road, is itself a position—a bias—so this argument is a justification for the bias rather than a denial of it. Second, the idea that the truth lies somewhere midway between the main opposed arguments is particularly ill founded. For example, Copernicus and Galileo said the earth went round the sun, while the Catholic Church said the sun circled the earth. The truth did not lie somewhere between the two. Thousands of survivors testify to the extermination of millions of Jews and others in the Nazi concentration camps; Holocaust deniers, like David Irving, claim this is a hoax. There is not some truth on both sides. Medical evidence suggested that cigarette smoking was a serious cause of cancer; the tobacco companies denied it for as long as they possibly could. They were not half right; they were lying. Moreover the tobacco companies cynically exploited the media notion that "balance" consists of sitting on the fence to hide the truth about smoking just as the oil companies and other vested interests are doing by financing climate scepticism at the moment.*

Given that the media cannot help but be biased the key questions are, what is the nature of that bias and how does it work?

## The nature of media bias

The media is not homogeneous. Nationally and internationally there is a multitude of different newspapers, TV stations, magazines, radio stations, individual programmes, film companies, films, record companies and so on, each of which has its own particular take on the world. In Britain there is the *Daily Telegraph* which is, as it has always been, closely allied to the Tory party. There is the *Sun* which was pro-Tory in the days of Thatcher, pro-Labour in the days of Blair and is now pro-Tory again (all at the behest of its owner, Rupert Murdoch), the *Daily Mirror* which is traditionally Labour (but right wing Labour), and the *Guardian* which is centre-left and liberal with a small "l". In the US there is Fox News, which is right wing and Republican (Rupert Murdoch again), and Hollywood, which is mostly liberal and Democrat. In Italy much of the media, including three national television channels and the country's largest publishing house, is owned by the prime minister, Silvio Berlusconi, and supports Silvio Berlusconi. Among French daily papers *Le Figaro* leans to the right, *Le Monde* slightly to the left. Obviously such an inventory could go on more or less forever, but I simply want to make the point that it is

---

* See Suzanne Jeffery, "Why We Should be Sceptical of Climate Sceptics", *International Socialism* 129 (winter 2011).

not part of my argument that there is some secret conspiracy or hidden power controlling all the media and ensuring that it follows some party line or specific agenda (as there was, very clearly, in Stalinist Russia, for example).

Colin Sparks has provided a very sophisticated and nuanced account of why these differences exist and how they work in his article "Inside the media" in *International Socialism* 98 (spring 2003).[9] However, I want to stress that there is one thing, one particular bias, that 95, no 99, percent of the media, both in Britain and in the world, has in common: it is pro-capitalist. This is so pervasive, so much the "natural" order of things, that it gets taken for granted. What I mean is that the overwhelming majority of the media simply assumes, without feeling any need to specifically argue the matter, that ordinary capitalist business activity is a legitimate, indeed desirable, thing. It assumes that if business in general is doing well, ie making high profits and expanding production, that is good for the nation and for us all. It assumes that business people are legitimate spokespeople on a wide range of topics, and that education ought, among other things, to be meeting the needs of business (it's usually called "the economy"). It assumes that if exports have risen that's good news, for us all, not just for the firms making money out of them; that if a firm opens up a factory or call centre it is "creating" or "providing" jobs; that if the stock market rises it is good news for us all, and if it falls it is bad news.

To illustrate this look at this extract from the article, "Inside the world of China's super-rich" by Nick Rosen, from the BBC News website, 7 June 2011:[10]

Who are the leaders of China's economic miracle? Where do they come from, and what are their wildest ambitions?

A hundred years ago it was the likes of Rockefeller, Ford, Carnegie who were building the future.

With China closing in on America to become the world's biggest economy, the next century belongs to names like...

Zong...Dai...Liu.

We had better get used to it.

As I read ever-more hyperbolic accounts of the Chinese economy, its impact on global trade, and the spending spree of its newly rich middle classes, I wanted to find out about the men and women who are leading this transformation...

I was not after the bosses in government and the Communist Party, although they are pulling the levers in their state-controlled society.

I was seeking the people behind the country's explosive economic growth—the top entrepreneurs.

They are the ones building world-beating companies, leading China's export success and creating new jobs by the million.

Thirty years ago the Party denounced entrepreneurs as: "self-employed traders and peddlers who cheat, embezzle, bribe and evade taxation".

Then the line changed. Deng Xiaoping, the driving force behind the move to capitalism after Mao's death, famously declared "to get rich is glorious"...

Karl Marx himself had a soft spot for entrepreneurs. In *Das Kapital* he asserted that workers were exploited by capitalists who profited from the added value of their labour.

But he argued entrepreneurs, although still capitalists, added their own value—through their fresh ideas and ability to seize opportunities.

Entrepreneurs, at least the good ones, were benign capitalists, said Marx. That explains their rehabilitation in post-Mao China...

I wanted to get behind the corporate announcements and the carefully managed public appearances to see how China's super-rich actually live, to hear what they really think and to try to understand why they had risen to the top of society, rather than their 1.3 billion fellow-countrymen and women.

What do they feel about the vast mass of China's population? How are they coping with their wealth? What are their plans for the future?

As they talked openly about their fortunes, their path to the top, their hopes for their own children, and the prospects for the world's fastest growing economy, I felt I had just begun to penetrate behind the mask of inscrutability which is the default mode for all Chinese dealings with foreigners.

As well as being fascinating characters in their own right, they allowed us to glimpse new China through their eyes, and understand the forces that will shape all our lives over the next decades.

The first thing to say about this article is that it has passed entirely without notice and I'm sure would have been regarded by both its author and by the BBC as politically uncontroversial and "unbiased". I chose it not because it is in any way unusual but precisely because of its innocuous typicality. In fact it is a sycophantic puff piece about these "super-rich" men (I cut out, for reasons of space, some of the slavering over their $50,000 watches and so on) which contains a crude stereotype about the Chinese "mask of inscrutability" and an outright falsehood about Marx— Marx neither "had a soft spot for entrepreneurs", nor argued in *Das Kapital*, which Rosen has clearly not read, that they "added their own value—through their fresh ideas and ability to seize opportunities".* But these are minor points. The main point is that the whole article is premised on, and absolutely takes for granted, the fundamental capitalist

---

* In reality Marx developed what is known as "the labour theory of value" which argued explicitly that all value derives from labour and not at all from the cleverness of entrepreneurs. It is a minor matter but I have noticed over the years that it is regarded as perfectly acceptable in most of the media to make up quotations or opinions and attribute them to Marx (or Lenin or Trotsky) virtually at will, without the least evidence or effort to check their truthfulness.

assumption that entrepreneurs, especially big entrepreneurs, are the principal creators of wealth, builders of world beating economies, and the people who will shape the future and "all our lives".

By the same token the media is almost entirely anti-socialist. I do not mean by this the "socialism" of Tony Blair or Ed Miliband which in reality completely accepts the continuation of capitalism and offers no threat at all to the system, but socialism which stands for the abolition of capitalism and the social ownership and control of production. Since the media assumes that capitalism is the natural order of things it also assumes that socialism is a strange and outlandish idea. Advocates of socialism very seldom get to appear in the media and when they do they are usually framed by the presenter as weird and possibly wicked. Articles or programmes discussing socialist ideas are even more rare and on the few occasions they do appear it is usually in marginal slots (11.30 at night, the odd column at the foot of an inside page). The media, as we have noted, is "moderate"; it stands in the middle of the road but it is a capitalist road, and socialists are seen as extremists and troublemakers, somewhat akin to highwaymen or roadside bandits.

Consider the following two (imaginary) versions of a report on the same event in the mouth of a six o'clock newsreader:

The German car manufacturer, Volkswagen, today announced plans to open a new plant in the Middlesbrough area creating 2,000 new jobs. Local community leaders welcomed the news, saying it would provide much needed investment and employment in a region hard hit by the recession.

The German car manufacturer, Volkswagen, today announced plans to open a new plant in the Middlesbrough area. They hope to exploit 2,000 workers. It appears they were attracted by the plentiful supply of cheap labour in the area and the opportunity it presents for high profits. Trade union leaders urged all new employees at the plant to join a union, saying the company was known for its ruthless labour relations.

The first version, which is the pro-capitalist view, sounds completely "normal" and unexceptional (as it is) and, crucially, it sounds neutral; in fact it presents Volkswagen as a social benefactor. The second version, the socialist view of the same event, sounds really strange and outlandish—it could not possibly be broadcast by the BBC or ITV—and it sounds biased, even though (in my opinion, of course) it is much closer to the truth than the first version.

## The causes of the bias

The main cause of this pro-capitalist anti-socialist bias is very simple. The vast bulk of the media, in Britain and in the world, consists of private capitalist businesses, in most cases very big businesses like Walt Disney, News Corporation, Viacom, Time Warner and Axel Springer AG, so naturally they support capitalism and business. It could be objected that the journalists, editors and producers who write the papers and make the TV or radio programmes are not capitalists and this would be true. But these media businesses are hierarchies, not democracies, and the journalists who work for them know what is required if they are to keep their jobs or get promotion.* Imagine you are a reporter for the *Sun*: you know that every story you submit goes to a sub-editor who checks and changes it, and you know that the sub-editor works for the editor and knows the style and political line desired by the editor and the editor knows the line required by the owner, Rupert Murdoch.

---

* For a fuller analysis of the details and complexities of these hierarchies see Colin Sparks, "Inside the Media", as above.

Anyone who wants to survive or prosper in the company has not only to accept being censored but has to learn very quickly to censor themselves.

Clearly there are exceptions to this. In many countries there are state run TV stations, by far the most significant of which is the BBC, which plays not only a national but also a certain world role. The BBC is a publicly, ie state, owned corporation financed by licence fee, which does not run to make a profit for shareholders and is governed by a charter that explicitly requires it to maintain political neutrality. Its national and international standing is bound up with its reputation for truthfulness and objectivity. But this "objectivity" means only that, unlike some state run TV stations, it is not simply a mouthpiece of the British government and the political neutrality means essentially that it adopts a stance roughly midway between the Tory and Labour front benches. All the arguments about pro-capitalist bias apply just as strongly to the BBC as they do to the rest of the media.

This is because the government is a part of the state, but only a part. The state is an interlocking network of institutions that stands above society and exercises ultimate legal authority over it including, crucially, a monopoly over the use of lawful violence. The central institutions of the state are the armed forces, the police, the judiciary, the prisons, and the upper reaches of the civil service (the people who run government ministries, etc, not the people who work in benefit offices or job centres). In Britain the head of state is nominally the queen—in most countries it is a more or less ceremonial president—but the people who actually run the state are not usually publicly identified as doing so.

The state in virtually every modern society claims to represent the nation "as a whole". It presents itself, and is normally presented in the media and the education system, as independent of any vested interest and serving the people, all the people. At one and the same time it claims to be the supreme political authority and "non-political". The armed forces fight "for the country". The police "serve the public". Judges are "independent". Civil servants work for "the elected government of the day".

This concept of the neutrality of the state is central to the claim that Britain and other Western capitalist societies are democracies; nevertheless it is a myth. Long ago, in *The Communist Manifesto* of 1848, Karl Marx wrote, "The executive of the modern state is but a committee for managing the common affairs of the whole bourgeoisie." Frederick Engels added, "The modern state, no matter what its form, is essentially a capitalist machine—the state of the capitalists, the ideal personification of the total national capital" (*Socialism: Utopian and Scientific*, 1880). Numerous theoretical and empirical research studies—most notably *The State in Capitalist Society* by Ralph Miliband (father of Ed)—and 160 years of experience have proved Marx and Engels correct on this. Whenever ordinary people have tried to resist the power of capitalist bosses or challenge the capitalist system, from early 19th century Chartists to the Paris Commune of 1871, from the General Strike of 1926 to the Miners' Strike of 1984-5, to the Greek and French workers' revolts and the Irish and British students in 2010, the state, in the shape of the police, the army and the courts, has been on hand to defend the system and the property of the rich. Frequently it has done this with great brutality, including killing and torture. Moreover, state run industries, such as the National Coal Board in the 1980s or British Rail before it was privatised, ran as capitalist industries, under capitalist management, competing with other firms to maximise their profits.

Thus the fact that the BBC is a state owned broadcaster does not eliminate its pro-capitalist bias, rather it guarantees it. The BBC is run by its director general who is its editor-in-chief. The current director general is Mark Thompson, educated at Stoneyhurst College and Merton College,

Oxford, and he is the highest paid public employee in Britain, earning between £800,000 and £900,000 a year. He has demonstrated his "impartiality" by, among other things, supporting the invitation to BNP leader Nick Griffin to appear on *Question Time*, and by refusing to broadcast the Disasters Emergency Committee Gaza Appeal for humanitarian aid. The director general is appointed by the BBC Trustees (until 2007 the Board of Governors) who in turn are appointed by the queen on the advice of government ministers. The person appointed director general will obviously be an experienced administrator with a proven record of being a responsible moderate, ie pro-capitalist—an active anti-capitalist or radical would never be appointed—but even so the trustees are there to intervene in the unlikely event that the director general turns "maverick" or "gets out of line", which means seriously contravenes the interests of the establishment, that is, the interests of capitalism.

How this operates was clearly demonstrated in the removal of director general Greg Dyke over the Gilligan/Kelly affair in 2004. This concerned the Blair government's claim (proven false) that Iraq had "weapons of mass destruction" in the run-up to the Iraq war of 2003. BBC journalist Andrew Gilligan produced a report saying that the government dossier claiming that intelligence sources showed Saddam Hussein possessed such weapons had been "sexed-up" by the government (specifically Alistair Campbell). His source was Dr David Kelly, a senior UN weapons inspector. When Gilligan came under attack from Campbell and the government Greg Dyke defended him. Then Kelly, under intense political, media and secret service pressure, was found dead. Tony Blair appointed Lord Hutton to lead a public inquiry into the affair, and when the Hutton Inquiry, in a blatant pro-government whitewash, condemned Gilligan and the BBC, the BBC governors withdrew their support from their director general and Dyke was forced to resign. Gilligan was dismissed.

The point is that the issues involved were important not just for the Blair government but for the British state and the British ruling class as a whole: it could not be openly admitted that the state had gone to war on a deliberate lie, even though this was manifestly the case. In such circumstances a director general and a journalist who failed to grasp where their "duty" lay could easily be dispensed with. Moreover the whole thing could be orchestrated through structures each of which claimed to be "independent", "impartial" and acting in "the public interest".

This does not mean the BBC is the same as the *Daily Mail* with an overt party bias. As an organisation it knows that there are two factors that work against open right wing bias: (1) that its national and international credibility depend on maintaining a certain appearance of neutrality; and (2) many of its best journalists, researchers, producers may personally have progressive views and they need to be given a certain leeway to keep them on board. The result of this balancing act is that the BBC is not a crude right wing propaganda outfit like Fox News, nor is it a Stalinist propaganda outfit like Russian TV in the Brezhnev era; rather it is, behind an impartial facade, a moderate pro-capitalist, pro-establishment propaganda outfit.

## The effect of the bias

The fact that only a minority of people are conscious socialists and that the debate between capitalism and socialism is not central to the political discourse in Britain does not mean that that the media's pro-capitalist bias has only a marginal effect on its output. On the contrary it is absolutely central to shaping its entire style and content.

In the first place this bias completely structures all the news and current affairs coverage. Thus massive priority is given to the words and deeds of top politicians over those of ordinary people. With the exception of certain special areas—crime, "celebrity" and sport—people's newsworthiness is ranked more or less in accordance with their standing in the capitalist class structure. Crime is an exception because the media treads very carefully where the crimes of the rich and powerful are concerned, especially given their ability to sue, but delights in lurid accounts of the crimes of the lower classes as this both enables them to paint ordinary people in a bad light, thus reinforcing the capitalist view of human nature as basically wicked, and fuels calls for "law and order" and more punitive sentences which strengthen the repressive powers of the state. Celebrity and sport, and sports stars are celebrities, are exceptions because one of their key functions is to persuade us that "ordinary people" can rise to the top, even though the overwhelming majority of celebs don't get anywhere near the *real* top of society. The current list of the UK's richest 100 people consists entirely of capitalists and contains not a single show business celebrity or sports star.

The pro-capitalist bias influences the whole process of story selection discussed at the beginning of this chapter. It determines the language used in reporting what the media calls "industrial relations" and socialists would call strikes or the trade union struggle. Thus wherever possible disputes and strikes are reported in terms of their "effects" on the public: if rail workers are on strike the media will try to interview disgruntled commuters who can't get home from work; if it is airline staff or air traffic controllers they will look for stranded holiday makers; and the disruption will always be laid at the door of the workers. In contrast the actual cause of the dispute, ie the workers' grievance, will, if they can get away with it, be left out of the report altogether so as to give the impression that the industrial action is just wilful bloody mindedness. If the issues must be covered the management will be said to be "offering" this or that or "appealing" for the other, especially for the workers to call off their "damaging" action, while the unions will be described as "rejecting the offer" or "demanding" x, y and z. Trade unions are regularly described as "having too much power" and "holding the country to ransom". The same is almost never said of employers despite the fact that they manifestly have much more power and wealth than trade unions and can, and do often, hold governments and workers to ransom by threatening to close down factories and move production elsewhere. And when it comes to industrial disputes even the very left wing end of the commercial media like the *Guardian* and the *Daily Mirror* are usually hostile to strikers and "militant" trade unionists. A mass of evidence to support the general assertions made here was collected by the Glasgow University Media Group in the 1970s (when industrial relations were continually at the centre of national news) and presented in three pioneering studies, *Bad News* (Glasgow Media Group, Routledge and Kegan Paul, 1976), *More Bad News* (Glasgow Media Group, Routledge and Kegan Paul, 1980) and *Really Bad News* (Glasgow Media Group, Writers and Readers Co-operative, 1982).

Left wing protest demonstrations get an equally rough ride. Here the media operate a very neat trick worthy of *Catch-22*. If the demonstration passes off peacefully, even if it is very large, it is often given almost no coverage at all. I have personally taken part in anti-racist and anti Iraq war marches of 100,000 people or more which were completely ignored by the press. If on the other hand there is some kind of trouble or "violence" the media will give the demo massive coverage but will focus entirely on condemning the demonstrators. At the same time they will emphasise that the "militants" responsible for the violence have damaged and distracted from the cause they were demonstrating for—which the media would otherwise have ignored.

My first personal experience of this was the anti Vietnam War demonstration of 27 March 1968 which culminated in a pitched battle between police and demonstrators in front of the US Embassy in Grosvenor Square. The newspapers launched a ferocious onslaught on the violence of the marchers. Apart from the fact that they never contemplated the possibility that the police (who used horses to charge the crowd) might have had something to do with do it, one might have thought that editors so appalled at the "violence" of some student battling with a mounted policeman might have had a problem with the "violence" of the US carpet-bombing and napalming Vietnamese villages. Apparently not. Similar media storms have been whipped up against demonstrators on many occasions since then including the SWP anti-fascists who broke up the National Front march in Lewisham in 1977, the miners' mass picket at Orgreave in 1984, the Poll Tax Riot of 1990, the Anti Nazi League confrontation with police when trying to march to BNP headquarters in Welling in 1993, and, of course, the recent student demos in November/December 2010. Moreover these storms invariably result in the identification and prosecution of individual protesters as well as preparing the ground for "exemplary" sentences.

The pro-capitalist bias shapes every panel on every discussion programme. On the most important of these, *Question Time*, the panel regularly consists of something like this: one Tory, one New Labour, one Liberal Democrat, one businessperson (often also a Tory), and one other. The first four of these are almost always supporters of capitalism (with the exception of very rare Labour left wingers) and the one other is often just an independent liberal from show business. Only very occasionally is the fifth place filled by an actual socialist or serious left winger. So there are usually two Tories, always a majority for capitalism, and supporters of capitalism outnumber socialists by about ten or 20 to one.

The bias also affects how interviews are conducted. A

quite different tone and manner is adopted when the interviewee is a "respected" mainstream politician from when he or she is the representative of some "extremist" or "disapproved of", ie anti-capitalist, cause. As soon as the interview starts the aggressive tone of voice signals to the audience that this is a "bad" person. From time to time the British establishment decides that some individual is a serious political threat. When that happens it is open season on that person as far as the media is concerned—more or less anything goes. Tony Benn and Ken Livingstone in the early 1980s, when there seemed to be a chance of Labour moving seriously to the left, Arthur Scargill at the time of the Great Miners' Strike and (to a slightly lesser extent) George Galloway over the Iraq war, were all subject to this kind of media demonisation. This may seem strange to younger readers of this booklet because now that he's no longer a threat Tony Benn is treated as a kindly uncle and national treasure, but for a few years he was portrayed as a dangerous lunatic.*

It is necessary to stress here that these observations do not imply a conspiracy theory. I am not suggesting that some secret centralised committee somewhere sends out an order, "Get Benn!" and everyone falls into line. This is not needed. Media people—successful journalists, editors, presenters, producers, etc get where they are partly through their ability to keep their finger on the pulse, to sense the mood, not so much among the general public, certainly not in the working class, but among the middle class and above all the establishment. They mix with powerful politicians and business people professionally and socially, at briefings, lunches, parties and so on, like Rebekah Brooks of News International and the Camerons in the "Chipping Norton Set". Professionally they

---

\* For a detailed account of the media demonisation of Tony Benn, see Glasgow University Media Group, *Really Bad News*, as above, pp67-112.

depend on tip offs, leaks and inside information and know what is wanted by their superiors. The likes of Trevor McDonald and Fiona Bruce, Anna Ford and Kirsty Wark also know when to sound happy and when to sound sombre, and every time they so much as raise an eyebrow out of line it will be noted.

Most importantly, the pro-capitalist bias is by no means limited to news and current affairs: rather it pervades the media as a whole. Think, for example, of programmes like *The Apprentice* and *Dragons' Den* that constitute more or less overt pro-business propaganda by celebrating "entrepreneurship". Obviously there are not going to be any "How to be a union rep" or "Young shop steward of the year" programmes. That would be ridiculous! But this only scratches the surface—the real problem is that capitalist values and a capitalist ethos permeate even the most avowedly apolitical and anti-political sections of the media such as light entertainment and advertising. I will discuss these areas in the next chapter.

# 2. Bread and circuses

The vast bulk of media output consists not of news coverage or educational material, but of "entertainment". It is designed to give people enjoyment and the expectation is that people will consume it not because they need to, or ought to, but because they want to. It ranges from the music industry pretty much as a whole, including radio stations mainly or wholly devoted to music, to films from Hollywood, Disney or Bollywood, to novels, children's comics, pornography, much of the TV schedules and a considerable part of newspapers (especially the so-called tabloids or popular press).

With significant exceptions such as John Berger's *Ways of Seeing* TV series from 1972, or Ken Loach's *Cathy Come Home* drama from 1966, this material is constructed so as to give pleasure without making too many intellectual or emotional demands and without causing too much upset. The assumption is that since most people do a hard day's work, outside or inside the home, and generally find life difficult and stressful, what they want from the media is "easy" listening, viewing or reading which offers either unproblematic excitement (say the average action movie) or gentle relaxation (say a chat show or family sitcom).

Since politics is pretty unpopular and widely considered bothersome—full of arguments, conflicts and difficult questions—this whole area of "entertainment" presents itself as non-political. In reality it is anything but. Of course it does not focus on the day in parliament or who to vote for in the next election, which is how politics is commonly defined, but what it does do, overwhelmingly, is present a view of the world from the standpoint of those who run and support capitalism. Once again the fact that it does so without acknowledging what it is doing, and mixes it in with ingredients which people do actually enjoy, only makes the ideological influence more powerful.

Take for example the *Sun*'s page 3 feature. This offers, primarily to its male readers, a modicum of voyeuristic sexual pleasure—the image of a conventionally attractive bare-breasted young woman. This is presented by the *Sun* as "just a bit of fun" and anyone who objects is denounced as a prude and a killjoy. Labour MP Clare Short, who campaigned against page 3 in 1986, was specifically branded "killjoy Clare" by the paper. In reality, as the *Sun* is well aware and most of its readers also sense, it encapsulates and, crucially, reinforces a whole conception of the social role and sexuality of women. It reduces women to their bodies, stripping them of their intelligence, personality and real emotions (the captions accompanying the image are part of this) and presents them as existing primarily for male gratification. In particular it encourages a specific, already existing, male way of talking about women in the canteen, the pub, etc, that is the discourse of "I'd give her one" and "I wouldn't kick her out of bed!" At the same time it puts pressure on women to seek to conform to these more or less unattainable standards of airbrushed "perfection".

Another, more complex, example is provided by the film *Titanic*. *Titanic* (made in 1997 and written and directed by James Cameron) was one of the biggest grossing films of all time, and I choose it because there is a good chance that readers of this book will have seen it. *Titanic* offered viewers a range of pleasures: the reconstruction of a famous episode in history; a very dramatic story; state of the art special effects; a glimpse of ruling class elegance and luxury; a romantic love story transgressing class boundaries. The last of these is a popular and recurring theme in literature from children's folk stories like *Cinderella* through Henry

Fielding's *Tom Jones* to D H Lawrence's *Lady Chatterley's Lover*, partly because it so rarely happens in real life. (The pleasures offered in popular culture are frequently those which the mass audience are deprived of in daily life—think of Fred Astaire musicals in the Depression of the 1930s, or James Bond movies). Embedded in these elements, however, is a highly political view of the world.

Born in a revolution against British colonialism in 1776, the United States of America has always presented itself as a land of freedom and opportunity—a friend of the oppressed. "Give me your tired, your poor, your huddled masses yearning to breathe free", said the Statue of Liberty to aristocratic Europe in the 19th century. And in the 19th century, despite slavery and racism, there was an element of truth in this, but the rhetoric was maintained through the 20th century when America became the world's leading imperialist power with a vast informal economic empire, into the Cold War and on into the "War on Terror". Immigrants are no longer welcome in the same way but the claim to embody "freedom" has been continually renewed. America has been aided in the propagation of this myth by not having a feudal past and hence no monarchy, no hereditary aristocracy, and no House of Lords. Thus despite being one of the most unequal societies in the world, with very deep class divisions, America has been able to maintain an image of itself as "classless".

*Titanic* systematically endorses this view of America. The ship sets sail from Southampton, bound for New York—a literal and metaphorical journey from the old world to the new. On board is Rose DeWitt Bukater (Kate Winslet), an upper class young woman, engaged to the even more upper class Cal Hockley. It is going to be, essentially, an arranged marriage to solve the Bukater family's debt problem. Rose is desperately unhappy and wants out. At one point she considers throwing herself overboard but is saved by another passenger, Jack

Dawson (Leonardo di Caprio), a poor itinerant artist from steerage, with whom she proceeds to fall in love and have an affair. Hockley, depicted as cold hearted, arrogant and vengeful, is enraged by this. He uses his valet to have Jack framed and manacled in the hold, and then tries, unsuccessfully, to shoot him. Rose and Jack escape the clutches of Cal but are unable to get into a lifeboat as the ship sinks. They end up in the sea, where Jack dies of the cold but Rose is rescued and goes on to a new, "free" life as an ordinary person (she renames herself Rose Dawson) in America.

This basic story of an escape from old, hidebound, unfeeling, aristocratic privilege to modern American freedom and equality is reinforced by a number of subordinate scenes and plot devices: the contrast between the cold rigid atmosphere on the upper deck and the relaxed, lively, spirited dancing below (which Rose joins); the evident snobbery towards Jack at the captain's table and the way it is countered by Molly Brown, who represents new American money; the fact that the evil Spicer Lovejoy (Cal's valet) is played by a very English actor, David Warner; and the crude class bias in the treatment of passengers as the *Titanic* sinks.

In other words *Titanic*, which was rewarded for its efforts with 11 Oscars, showed America to itself and to the world in exactly the way that its economic and political establishment would choose. Clearly this kind of analysis could be repeated for innumerable mass media cultural artefacts. However, it should be noted, as I did at the start of chapter 1, that this material is not politically homogeneous. Some of what emerges from Hollywood and the American culture industry is unambiguously right wing, the cultural equivalent of George Bush and the Republican Party—the *Rambo* movies for example—but generally speaking Hollywood is mildly liberal in the sense that Steven Spielberg and Barack Obama, Paul Newman and Ted Kennedy are liberals; occasionally it is more radically liberal as in some Oliver Stone movies or

*The Daily Show with Jon Stewart* on TV. Only Michael Moore (of *Bowling for Columbine*, *Fahrenheit 9/11* and *Capitalism: A Love Story*) springs to mind as genuinely left wing, and even Moore says at the end of *Capitalism: A Love Story*, "There is an alternative to capitalism, it's called… democracy"—not socialism.

But given the vast amount of material involved exhaustive analysis is impossible. What I want to do, therefore, is work towards establishing a general case by looking at two mass media genres, each of which plays an important role in contemporary culture—game shows and soap operas—and then examine the effects of advertising, which runs through, sustains and influences most contemporary media.

## Game shows

Game shows of one kind or another have been part of radio and television since the start and have developed as these media have developed. Wikipedia's list of UK game shows[11] comes in at 146 and they are arranged by genre so we can see that they include 31 quizzes, six dating shows and 13 so-called "reality" shows. Obviously these shows are presented and generally regarded as completely "non-political" except when they become "political" by virtue of some scandal attaching to them, eg the racism scandal with Jade Goody and Shilpa Shetty in *Celebrity Big Brother 2007*, which produced a motion in the House of Commons and demonstrations in India, or when a politician appears in them such as the unfortunate George Galloway in *Celebrity Big Brother 2006*. Equally obviously game shows are (a) intrinsically capitalist enterprises, produced and run to make money through advertising, commercial sponsorship and sale to TV stations—Endemol, the maker of *Big Brother* and the equally successful *Deal or No Deal*, was bought by Telefonica for €5.5 billion in 2000 (though subsequently had to be sold at a loss when its fortunes declined); and (b) totally dominated by a thoroughly capitalist ethos and value system.

The essence of game shows is that they consist of people competing to win prizes. The games they compete in range from more or less pure chance (*Play Your Cards Right* or *Deal or No Deal*) to some kind of knowledge quiz (*Who Wants to Be a Millionaire?*) to the more physical (*Gladiators* or *Total Wipeout*). The prizes vary from consumer goods (this was more common in the 1950s and 1960s) to cash, to career opportunities (especially in talent shows like *The X Factor*). Usually the contestants are "ordinary" people without professionally developed knowledge or skills. The idea is that the audience, other "ordinary" people, will identify with the contestants and enjoy imagining that they are winning the car, the holiday or the money. Interestingly, in *Mastermind*, the most "intellectual" and up market game show, aimed more or less explicitly at a middle class audience, there are no money prizes; status or kudos is supposed to be its own reward. The same applies to *University Challenge*.

Of course all this competitiveness is supposed to be just human nature. Now whether or not there is an element of competiveness in human nature is a complex debate, which I won't rehearse here, but the intense focus on it in game shows is very much a reflection of capitalism as an economic system. Capitalism is driven by competition between businesses rather than by cooperation between producers—even though cooperation between producers is an indispensable prerequisite of human production—and therefore capitalist ideology, in education and in work, puts huge emphasis on competition as opposed to cooperation. Thus in our education system assessment is organised on a competitive basis and collaboration is generally condemned as "cheating".

In some game shows the encouragement of capitalist consumerism is blatant and extreme. The audience is set up to "Ooh!" and "Ah!" at the prizes or even whoop and scream in mock ecstasy when someone wins. In others the contestants are required to make fools of themselves or even be humiliated or risk humiliation for the privilege of appearing on TV, which reinforces the idea that the capitalist culture industry is king and all must bow down before it.

In recent years the most culturally important game show has been *Big Brother*. *Big Brother* inserted a number of new elements into the well-established game show genre. In the first place it was touted as an example of "reality TV". In the second participants competed on the basis not of skills, even trivial ones, but "popularity" with the public. Third, the prize was not so much money as "celebrity". Each of these elements needs to be examined.

The claim to define "reality" or to be representing it is in itself a political claim. This is true at the level of philosophy, at the level of history, sociology and economics, and at the level of media discourse. How often do you hear a TV presenter or journalist or panellist on a discussion programme say "in the real world" or "as someone who works in the real world"? And doesn't it usually turn out that what they mean by this is the world of business, capitalist business as opposed to say the academic world or even the world of politics (parliamentary politics). Moreover they mean the world of business from the point of view of the owners, not the workers. In the case of "reality TV" the claim is that we will be watching "ordinary people" as they actually live their lives, as opposed to actors or performers, such as you would see in a drama or sitcom.

This claim is completely misleading. The participants in *Big Brother* are under intense surveillance by millions and know it and are competing to win: they are therefore performing from day one and far from being "everyday life" the circumstances in which they are performing are completely artificial and highly controlled by the programme makers. The level of control exercised in the making of TV programmes, especially *Big Brother*, is carefully masked and commonly underestimated by the public. This control begins with choosing the participants. Rather than being just "ordinary" people they are specially selected from a huge number of applicants on the basis that they will produce "good television", ie generate drama and conflict. Then they are subject to all sorts of tricks and manipulation, like cutting their food rations, to put them under pressure and set them against each other. At the same time there is time delay in broadcasting, so the output is censored, not just for swearing or libel but also for "politics", ie to prevent participants putting over their political ideas.

The fact that the *Big Brother* participants compete in terms of popularity is particularly significant. Moreover this competition has a double character: on the one hand they have to try to be popular with their fellow inmates in the house to avoid nomination for eviction, and on the other they have to please the general viewing audience to avoid being voted out if they are nominated. To survive in the contest, therefore, they have to "sell" their personality in two different directions at once: to be both deeply conformist so as not offend inmates or voters and to be "different" so as to stand out from the crowd.

The winner of *Big Brother* received a cash prize (usually about £100,000, ie a substantial but not huge amount) but the real prize was "celebrity". Celebrity is similar to fame—being heard of by large numbers of people—but also different. Fame has been around for thousands of years: Alexander the Great, Shakespeare, Napoleon and Marx were, and are, famous, but famous for something—conquering half the known world or writing great plays. Celebrity is a relatively new phenomenon and closely linked to the modern mass media. Celebrity, of course, is hierarchical and at its lower levels—the so-called C and D list celebs—is a matter of being famous just for being famous; it involves no significant talent or achievement. Whole magazines such as *OK!*, *Hello!* and *Heat* are devoted to celebrity, but at its heart lies television, the still dominant mass medium. Someone who has appeared on TV a few times is more or less the definition of a celebrity. Appearing on TV, even as a weather presenter, makes you a fit subject for gossip in the magazines and other career opportunities such as opening supermarkets and getting a part in the Christmas pantomime, where you will be billed as "As seen on TV".

Just being in *Big Brother*, therefore, is the first step on the road to celebrity. Winning, it is hoped (though the hope is not always realised), offers a ticket of at least temporary entry into celebrity status. Losing spectacularly often works just as well, as in the cases of "Nasty Nick" Bateman and Jade Goody.

Lower grade celebrity has the advantage of seeming attainable to young working class people, to the "ordinary" people who made up the majority of *Big Brother* and other "reality" show contestants and audiences, but it comes at a price. Celebrities on the lower rungs have to be willing and ready for their private lives to become public property; indeed if they wish to remain celebs they have, like Jordan and Peter Andre, to positively offer up blow by blow accounts of their personal lives to the media vultures who alternately prey and parasite on them.

However, it is also the case that *Big Brother* is part of the process of humiliation and degradation which the trashier end of modern media inflicts on members of the public who become engaged with it. Anther particularly unpleasant example is *The Jeremy Kyle Show* which specialises in holding up to scorn the lives of members of the so-called "underclass", much as Hogarth recorded the inmates of Bedlam being paraded for the gentry in the 18th century—the difference being that the Bedlam inmates were incarcerated and displayed against their will, whereas Kyle's "guests" and *Big Brother* participants are avid volunteers willing to swap humiliation for the chance to appear on the great god, television.

With all this in mind it is worth asking what made *Big Brother* so popular (at least until the formula grew stale); what did the audience get out of it? As in any game show there was clearly an element of identification with the ordinary Joe winning the coveted prize, while at the same time it could also be argued there is an element of schadenfreude, of pleasure in the misfortunes of those who come a cropper in one way or another. However, more important than either of these factors, is, I believe, the way in which people used the programme as a means of negotiating and discerning the norms of acceptable social behaviour. This is very much the same as the way in which they use soap operas. They observe certain behaviour on the programme—Nick Bateman's cheating, Jade Goody's racism and ignorance, Brian Dowling's homosexuality—and how it is received by the other housemates. Then, crucially, they discuss it with family, friends and workmates. This process was latterly deliberately fostered by the creation of the discussion programme, *Big Brother's Little Brother*.

Two features of the *Big Brother* formula that I have already commented on are important here: first the illusion of "reality" and second that the competition is in terms of popularity. Thus viewers come to believe that by watching and discussing the programme they are learning how to avoid being socially ostracised and how to win popularity. And it is because they use it in this way that the ideology imbedded in the construction and control of the house and the programme as a whole is significant.

What is that ideology? Unsurprisingly it is pro-capitalist liberal individualism. Thus people who model their behaviour on the *Big Brother* pattern will compete with one another as individuals for fame and fortune. They will compete "fairly", which means they will not form any pacts or alliances with others; they will compete according to the rules of the game which are given from the outset and not question those rules. They will not discriminate in any way on grounds of race or sexuality (though a degree of sexism is OK, or more OK than racism or homophobia) but beyond this they will have no political ideas of any kind or if they do will certainly not talk about them. Above all they will not, and will not be able to, combine or unite against the tyranny of Big Brother. In other words this is more or less a carbon copy of the dominant ideology in early 21st century Britain.

I am not claiming that "embedding" this ideological stance in the game was either deliberate or the principal driver of the programme. The aim of the programme would simply have been to make money (by attracting a large audience) and the implicit ideology would have seemed "obvious" and "natural" to the programme makers. In all likelihood the only real debate would have been in the area of "identity"—race, gender and sexuality—and the issues would have been: (a) how to relate to a young contemporary audience; and (b) how to avoid getting into trouble with the regulatory authorities.

## Soap opera: the case of EastEnders

**TV ratings, w/e 29 May 2011**

| BBC1 | Millions |
|---|---|
| 1. *EastEnders* (Mon 20.02) | 9.73 |
| 2. *EastEnders* (Tue 19.30) | 9.06 |
| 3. *EastEnders* (Thu 19.29) | 8.86 |
| 4. *The Apprentice* (Wed 21.00) | 8.62 |
| 5. *EastEnders* (Fri 19.59) | 7.79 |
| 6. *Doctor Who* (Sat 18.45) | 6.72 |
| 7. *Waterloo Road* (Wed 19.29) | 6.12 |
| 8. *Ten O'Clock News* (Tue 22.00) | 5.74 |
| 9. *Holby City* (Tue 20.02) | 5.31 |
| 10. *Ten O'Clock News* (Mon 22.00) | 5.30 |

| ITV1 | Millions |
|---|---|
| 1. *Britain's Got Talent* (Sun 19.30) | 9.88 |
| 2. *Coronation Street* (Mon 20.30) | 9.38 |
| 3. *Coronation Street* (Mon 19.33) | 9.31 |
| 4. *Coronation Street* (Fri 20.29) | 8.49 |
| 5. *Coronation Street* (Thu 20.31) | 8.38 |
| 6. *Scott & Bailey* (Sun 21.02) | 8.31 |
| 7. *Coronation Street* (Fri 19.32) | 8.30 |
| 8. *Coronation Street* (Sun 19.01) | 7.59 |
| 9. *Emmerdale* (Thu 20.00) | 7.36 |
| 10. *UEFA Champions League Live* (Sat 18.59) | 7.23 |

As the above TV ratings for the week 22-29 May 2011 show, soap operas—specifically *EastEnders* and *Coronation Street*—retain their position as the dominant genre within television which in turn is the dominant mass medium. The most obvious explanation for this popularity is that ordinary working class people are able to identify with characters in these soaps, with their lives, their hopes and their problems, because these characters are "ordinary working class people" like themselves. In other words, as with the reality TV we have just been looking at, there is a claim or attribution of "realism" being made here. As *EastEnders* co-creator Julia Smith put it, "We don't make life; we reflect it".[12]

The realistic representation of everyday life, in the literal sense, in a soap opera or any other drama, is obviously impossible—apart from anything else "real life" takes place in real time and is mostly far too uneventful to serve as entertainment—but this is not what is meant, of course. Frederick Engels once wrote, "Realism, to my mind, implies, besides truth of detail, the truthful reproduction of typical characters under typical circumstances".[13]

By this criterion *Coronation Street* and *EastEnders* are far more realistic than the vast bulk of programming on television, including and particularly so-called reality TV. The characters are "ordinary people", not impossibly virtuous heroes, or rich fantasy figures as in various American soaps, or glamorous upper middle classes as in *Sex and the City*, or excessively comfortable and cosy as in *Friends*. They are set in contemporary Britain as opposed to some nostalgic imaginary past—be it of Jane Austen, Agatha Christie or *Upstairs, Downstairs*. Importantly, they are urban in location, which is where the majority of British people have lived since the middle of the 19th century, despite the persistent tendency to represent England and "Englishness" as quintessentially rural and village based. (This tendency goes back to the paintings of Constable, the myths of fox hunting and cricket on the village green, and is heavily represented in the media by *The Archers*, *Midsomer Murders*, *Miss Marple* and much else.) The dramatic intensity of life is highly exaggerated to provide cliffhanger endings which keep the viewer hooked, and the themes of these crises focus on the characters' family lives and personal relationships. Even so they are more balanced and "realistic" than the one-sided concentration on crime, inherent in the genre, of cop shows (even "ultra-realist" *The Wire*) and the one-sided focus on illness equally inherent in medical dramas.

This relative realism enables the viewer to use these programmes in a way that parallels the use made of *Big Brother*. That is, in watching the programmes and, importantly, in discussing them with family, friends, workmates, etc, viewers are able to use them as a sounding board by which to judge standards of conduct, norms of behaviour, in times when these are changing rapidly. How should we react to divorce, infidelity, domestic violence, teenage pregnancy, having a member of the family or community who is gay or diagnosed HIV positive and so on? Moreover it should be said that the makers of these programmes are very conscious of this function and consequently of their "responsibilities" in these matters. The storyline in *EastEnders* in the 1990s of Mark

Fowler being HIV-positive is summed up on Wikipedia as follows:

> Mark became the first mainstream soap character to be diagnosed as HIV-positive. The storyline came after a government request to "spread the word". Mark's story also helped dispel the myth that HIV is an automatic death sentence. He lived with the condition for 13 years before dying of an AIDS related illness. The Terrence Higgins Trust worked with the production team for the duration of Mark's story. Despite all the public health campaigns concerning HIV transmission, the biggest peak in requests for testing in Britain was seen in January 1991 when Mark Fowler was diagnosed HIV-positive. Carty [the actor who played Mark Fowler] has commented: "I feel that the storyline educated people at a time when there were lots of misconceptions about HIV and Aids… My main concern was that they'd get it right and, overall, I think they did—because it showed someone living with HIV, as opposed to dying of it".[14]

The more recent storyline involving child abuse in the family was praised by the NSPCC for raising awareness "of the hidden nature of sexual abuse". It is precisely this function as a kind of moral arbiter that makes some of the ways in which these programmes depart from "realism" of particular ideological significance. Three points about *EastEnders* illustrate this.

First, its main characters are not working class. The East End of London is a predominantly working class area and *EastEnders* is generally assumed to predominantly feature working class characters and represent working class life. In fact the majority of its central characters are small business people. Den and Angie Watts owned and ran the Queen Vic, as did Peggy Mitchell and now Kat and Alfie Moon. Phil Mitchell runs a garage and a nightclub. Ian Beale is an "entrepreneur" with a chippy and a market stall. The Branning brothers own a car dealership and a boxing gym. Even 19 year old Whitney Dean runs a market stall. Those characters who do have working class jobs, ie are employed wage workers, like Ricky Butcher or Carol Branning, generally work for the business people listed above or other small local firms, like Dot Cotton in the launderette. Although Masood Ahmed is employed as a postal worker this is very much in the background compared to the family's ownership of a food stall and a restaurant.

This is a significant misrepresentation not only of life in the East End but of life in Britain as a whole. Nationally the self-employed make up approximately 12 percent of the workforce; in London it is slightly higher at 15 percent, but still a very small minority. One of the reasons for this distortion is doubtless the dramatic requirement of the programme that all its characters should be known to each other and to the audience (whereas the reality of life in a big city is that you often don't know your next door neighbours, never mind all the people who live in your street or square). However, the effect of it is that *EastEnders* systematically excludes what is a major part of the life experience of the majority of people in modern capitalist society, namely waged employment for an employer (predominantly a medium sized or big employer) who they are not related to and do not know personally.

In this way *EastEnders*, despite its reputation, continues rather than challenges the pervasive underrepresentation of working class people in our culture that stretches all the way from Hollywood movies to the novel.

The second point is the underrepresentation of ethnic minorities. Precisely because the East End has long been working class and poor, it has also, since the Huguenots in the 17th century and the Irish and Jews in the 19th century, been an area of high immigration. It is now the most multicultural community in the United Kingdom. Since neither Albert Square nor Walford are real places *EastEnders* has no actual location, but it is clearly set somewhere in the region of the boroughs of Hackney and Tower Hamlets. Let us look briefly at the ethnic make-up of the populations of these boroughs.

Hackney is made up of 48.45 percent White British, 13.36 percent Other White (total white 61.81 percent), Asian (Indian, Pakistani, Bangladeshi, Chinese, etc) approximately 12 percent, and Black (Black British, Caribbean and African) approximately 22.5 percent. There are also about 7 percent Charedi (Hasidic or Ultra Orthodox) Jews, and 6 percent Turkish and Kurdish who are often subsumed in the "white" categories.[15] Tower Hamlets is 44 percent White British, 8 percent Other White (total white 52 percent) and 30 percent Bangladeshi.[16] This compares to UK figures of 92 percent White and 7.9 percent ethnic minorities with approximately 4.4 percent Asian and 2 percent Black.[17]

Clearly the ethnic minority population of the East End is massively underrepresented in *EastEnders*. In 2002 a study by the Commission for Racial Equality found that over four weeks the average proportion of visible minority faces on *EastEnders* was 9 percent. Is this underrepresentation racist? Objectively of course it is. The most probable explanation for it, in my view, is the producers' attribution to their audience (which is national) of a degree of "mild" racism which would lead them not to identify with or watch a programme in which nearly half the characters were non-white, rather than any deliberate intention to discriminate. Nevertheless what it signifies is that, faced with a perceived choice between reasonably accurate representation of ethnic minorities and the success of their programme (defined by ratings), the former is sacrificed for the latter.

This choice also has a major effect on the way in which the ethnic minority characters who do appear are represented. I do not mean by this whether or not the non-white characters are presented in a positive light, but the fact that they are generally depicted as isolated families rather than as part of a community or social network of other Bangladeshis, West Indians, or Turks. The only "community" we see in *EastEnders* is a white one, within which non-whites are "accepted" or integrated. This leads also to the reduction of the problem of racism to individual responses (more or less accepting, more or less tolerant) by the white characters, thus avoiding many of the main forms in which racism is experienced by ethnic minorities: institutionalised racism by the police, the courts, the education system, employers, the immigration authorities and so on. There is hardly a problem to do with sex and sexuality that *EastEnders* has not "boldly" tackled at some point but the issue of racism, which is and always has been of huge political significance in the actual East End, is largely swept under the carpet.

These failures to represent working class and ethnic minority experience lead directly to the third key point: *EastEnders* presents an almost totally depoliticised picture of life in the East End and, by implication, of working class life in Britain. In the 26 years of its existence the closest it has come to a serious political story line was in 2009 when the pub-owning, and therefore middle class, Peggy Mitchell stood for the council as an "independent", which was accompanied by advice in a video blog from Alastair Campbell (!) and a guest appearance by Boris Johnson (!!)* As far as I am aware there has never been a single significant character with left wing political views.

Now it is certainly true that most of the time the majority of ordinary people, middle class or working class, are not "into" politics, ie politics is not a serious focus of their lives.

---

* I presume this was the BBC's idea of political balance: one Labour, one Tory—two right wingers.

But it is also true that most people have some sort of political outlook and that the working class as a whole always contains at least a minority of left wingers, socialists, militant trade unionists and activists. Unless this was the case there could never have been a trade union and labour movement (or a far left) in Britain—all of which have manifestly existed. Moreover the East End of London has long been a particularly politicised area which has played a major role in the history of the British labour movement, not least in anti-fascist and anti-war struggles. Examples of this include: the match girls' strike of 1888 and the dockers' tanner strike of 1889; Sylvia Pankhurst and the East End Suffragettes; George Lansbury and Poplar council; the legendary Battle of Cable Street in 1936 when the people of the East End, led largely by the Communist Party, stopped an attempted march by Mosley's fascists; the great dockers' strike of 1972 that secured the release of the Pentonville Five; and the Anti Nazi League/Rock against Racism Carnival with the Clash in 1978. Moreover this is a tradition which has continued during the period covered by EastEnders and up to the present. 1986 saw police battling pickets at Wapping; in 2003 the East End came out massively against the Iraq War; in August 2011 there were riots in Hackney and Bethnal Green and on 3 September 2011 the English Defence League was stopped from marching through Tower Hamlets.

Yet none of this ever appears in *EastEnders*, either as past or present. This refusal to deal with politics is not politically neutral. What it does is leave existing politics, ie capitalist politics, completely unchallenged. A "non-political" working class is exactly what the capitalist class dreams of. And in providing it *EastEnders* is not only typical of soap operas, but of all television drama, and of the mass media as a whole. Of course there is the odd exception, but the rareness of the exceptions really does prove the rule.

## Advertising

Advertising pervades our lives and is increasingly unavoidable in modern urban life. This has two effects. First, there is the direct impact on the media and the choices its producers make. Edward Herman and Noam Chomsky assign an important role to advertising in their "propaganda model" of the functioning of the mass media, developed in *Manufacturing Consent*. They rank it as the second of five "filters" (the others are the size and wealth of media ownership, the reliance of the media on government and business as sources of information, "flak"—hostile comment and action by the powerful—as a means of disciplining the media, and "anti-communism" as a national religion and control mechanism) which, they argue, ensure and enforce the massive pro-capitalist bias of the media.

Herman and Chomsky are clearly correct in this. The main advertisers in the mass media are the big corporations because only they can afford mass advertising campaigns. For most of the mass media, advertising is their main source of revenue. In the cases of commercial television, radio, Facebook, Twitter and You Tube, it is close to the only source. In the case of newspapers and magazines, income derived from advertising far outweighs income from sales. As Herman and Chomsky argue, this has two main effects.

First it makes it almost impossible for independent or anti-capitalist media to compete with corporate, pro-capitalist media in the market place. The latter will inevitably receive the vast bulk of advertising while the former will receive little if any. This in turn enables the corporate media to operate with much higher production values, much superior distribution systems and, crucially, to sell titles or services at prices that are far below cost of production or, increasingly, to give them away for free.

Anti-capitalist media without comparable advertising revenue cannot match this. It also means that relatively low circulation titles aimed at affluent, up-market readers with high purchasing power can be more attractive to advertisers (and therefore more profitable) than higher circulation titles aimed at poorer working class readers.

A good example of how this has worked in practice (cited by Herman and Chomsky but based on the account in James Curran and Jean Seaton, *Power without Responsibility: The Press and Broadcasting in Britain*, London, 1985) is provided by the history of the *Daily Herald*. The *Herald* began in 1910 as the daily strike bulletin of the printers' union, the London Society of Compositors. It then developed, with the backing of dockers' leader Ben Tillett, left Labour politician George Lansbury, and other radical trade unionists, into a permanent labour movement daily. In 1922 the TUC took over the paper and it served as their official organ until 1929. In 1930 the TUC sold a 51 percent stake in the paper to Odhams Press, publishers of the *People*, but it retained its broadly pro labour movement orientation. By 1933 it was possibly the largest selling newspaper in the world and by 1964 with 4.7 million readers "the *Daily Herald* actually had almost double the readership of the *Times*, the *Financial Times* and the *Guardian* put together".[18] But with 8.1 percent of national daily circulation it received only 3.5 percent of net advertising revenue and in 1964 it was forced to close. It was relaunched as the *Sun*, and taken over by Murdoch in 1969—with consequences known to all. Similar fates befell Britain's two other left inclined mass circulation newspapers, the *News Chronicle* and *Reynolds News*. The *Chronicle*, which supported the Liberal Party, closed in 1960 and was taken over by the right wing *Daily Mail*. The weekly *Reynolds News* (later *Sunday Citizen*) was linked to the Co-operative Party, which in turn was affiliated to the Labour Party. It was forced to close in 1967.

Second, the dependence of both TV and newspapers on advertising gives major advertisers (ie big corporations) a de facto virtual veto on political content. If a media outlet broadcasts or publishes material not to the advertiser's liking it requires only a phone call to cancel the contract. (This, of course, is not censorship in any form—heaven forbid!—since corporations naturally have a perfect right to spend their money as they see fit.) Herman and Chomsky give a good example of this:

> Public television station WNET lost its corporate funding from Gulf + Western in 1985 after the station showed the documentary *Hungry for Profit*, which contains material critical of multinational corporate activities in the Third World. Even before the programme was shown, in anticipation of negative corporate reaction, station officials "did all we could to get the programme sanitised" (according to one station source). The chief executive of Gulf + Western complained to the station that the programme was "virulently anti-business if not anti-American", and that the station's carrying the programme was not the behaviour "of a friend" of the corporation. The London *Economist* says that "Most people believe that WNET would not make the same mistake again".[19]

The most important sentence here is the last one from the *Economist*, and the key point is not how often this power is exercised, but that most of the time it does not need to be. It needs only to be there as a threat for it to be internalised by all those working in the media. Just as the journalist working for the *Sun* knows what the editor wants and the editor knows what Rupert Murdoch wants, so all three know what their advertisers want and especially what they don't want, which is anything damaging to their specific interests or anything "anti-business" as such.

However, in addition to this more or less direct influence

on news and current affairs coverage there is an even more important way in which advertising shapes the media and, via the media, our whole cultural environment. This is through the fact that adverts themselves make up a very large part of media output and constitute a considerable proportion of the totality of visual images that we see in our lives as a whole. In between and interspersed through every TV programme and radio programme (with the exception of the BBC and other public service broadcasters) there are adverts; running through every newspaper, every colour supplement, every magazine are adverts; on every billboard on the streets of every town and city, in every shopping mall, in every train and bus station and every hotel reception, round the perimeter of every football stadium and the backs of every footballer, on the chassis of every racing car and everywhere else in this society where people are likely to gather, there are adverts. And in addition to its specific content, trying to persuade us to buy this or that product, each advert constitutes, almost without exception, an advertisement for capitalism.

One of the best explanations of this was provided by John Berger in the last chapter of his great book on art, *Ways of Seeing* (1972). I will offer some selected quotations (note that what I have called advertising Berger calls "publicity"):

In the cities in which we live, all of us see hundreds of publicity images every day of our lives. No other kind of image confronts us so frequently.

In no other form of society in history has there been such a concentration of images, such a density of visual messages.

One may remember or forget these messages but briefly one takes them in, and for a moment they stimulate the imagination by way of either memory or expectation…

We are now so accustomed to being addressed by these images that we scarcely notice their total impact...we accept the total system of publicity images as we accept an element of climate...

Publicity is usually explained and justified as a competitive medium which ultimately benefits the public (the consumer) and the most efficient manufacturers—and thus the national economy. It is closely related to certain ideas about freedom: freedom of choice for the purchaser: freedom of enterprise for the manufacturer... Publicity, it is thought, offers a free choice.

It is true that in publicity one brand of manufacture, one firm, competes with another; but it is also true that every publicity image confirms and enhances every other...to make the same general proposal. Within publicity, choices are offered between this cream and that cream, that car and this car, but publicity as a system only makes a single proposal.

It proposes to each of us that we transform ourselves, or our lives, by buying something more...

Publicity increasingly uses sexuality to sell any product or service...the good life in which you can buy whatever you want. To be able to buy is the same thing as being sexually desirable.

Publicity turns consumption into a substitute for democracy. The choice of what one eats (or wears or drives) takes the place of significant political choice. Publicity helps to mask and compensate for all that is undemocratic within society... But its offer is as narrow as its references are wide. It recognises nothing except the power to acquire...

Capitalism survives by forcing the majority, whom it exploits, to define their own interests as narrowly as possible*.[20]

These lines were written in 1972. They have become even more true and relevant over the past four decades. In *No Logo* Naomi Klein shows that total annual advertising expenditure in the United States rose from $50 billion in 1979 to nearly $200 billion in 1998,[21] and it is currently estimated at $300 billion, and, as Klein also shows, this has been particularly associated with and driven by the big corporations (Nike, Gap, Tommy Hilfiger, etc) and the rise of branding. Propaganda for these giant companies is propaganda for capitalism.

The normalisation of advertising, referred to by Berger above, disguises its totalitarian character. In the face of this it is necessary to make some simple points. First, while the occasional article written from an anti-capitalist point of view (by a John Pilger or a Seumas Milne) appears in the mainstream press, and very occasionally such people get to appear on *Question Time* or *Newsnight*, there are no anti-capitalist adverts. This is ensured not by conspiracy but simply by economics. They have the money; we do not. Similarly the corporations can cover a city in billboard posters advertising this or that commodity. Anyone who wants to advertise an anti-capitalist cause or event probably has to (illegally) flypost—again simple economics.

Second, the culture of advertising is a culture of systematic lying. Since this is largely ignored, or passed over in silence, it needs emphasising. Advertising involves deliberate planned deception of people. Of course much of the time it lies by suggestion rather than legally provable falsehoods,

---

* What Berger writes can be compared to Marx's extraordinary analysis of "The Power of Money" in his *Economic and Philosophical Manuscripts of 1844*: http://www.marxists.org/archive/marx/works/1844/manuscripts/power.htm

but legally provable or not they are falsehoods. Products are advertised as new when they are not new at all; food is advertised as homemade when it is clearly not. If there are six brands of washing powder they cannot all wash whitest. Every car insurance company promises savings—savings on what? On what you could spend with every other insurance company. Airlines offer headlines of cheap flights—from only £9.99! From is the key word—there is one flight at £9.99 at 4am when it will cost you £50 to get to the airport and before taxes, booking charges, baggage charges and the rest bring the price up to £60. These and a thousand other deceits become taken for granted.

What is more, the language of advertising—lying to people to get your hands on their money—is hailed as a virtue. Under the name of "marketing", it becomes something we are all supposed to do. Politicians should market themselves, with advertising slogans like "Ready for Change" or "Yes we can!" or "Let's get back to work!" Universities and colleges must market themselves with claims that they are "nationally and internationally recognised centres of excellence" (when they are nothing of the kind). Charities should market themselves to get a bigger share of the charity market.

Of course there are contradictions in this, as there are in the influence of the media generally (see chapter 4), eg the consumerism fed by advertising can lead to deep-seated and explosive rage among those who can't afford the commodities dangled in front of their noses, "as seen on TV", in the looting in the riots of August 2011. However, the overall effect of advertising is to reinforce the pro-capitalist bias that pervades the media.

# 3. Only giving them what they want

The idea that media news coverage is politically neutral or merely "reports the facts" will not withstand a moment's serious consideration; likewise, as we have seen, the notion that light entertainment is non-political or outside of politics. However, apologists for the media have at their disposal a more sophisticated argument: they can claim that the political values purveyed by the media, explicitly and implicitly, are not something the media industry imposes on the public but rather a reflection of the politics and values already held by the public. In other words they are "only giving people what they want".

This is the argument I would use if I were Rupert Murdoch being questioned by a critical interviewer. I would say, "The *Sun* is the bestselling newspaper in Britain. It sells three million copies a day. In contrast the *Guardian* sells less than 300,000. As for the so-called left wing papers which claim to represent the workers, I doubt if they sell 30,000 a week. No one forces people to buy the *Sun*. They buy it because they like it, because the *Sun*'s values are their values." It is also clear that this argument, if it is accepted, will serve to justify virtually all the mass media output—Fox News, *The X Factor*, *Nuts* and *Bizarre*, everything—providing only that it is popular.

Let us acknowledge that there is some truth in this argument. If a large pile of *Sun* newspapers were to be placed on the counter of a newsagents next to an equally large pile of *Socialist Worker* or the *Morning Star* and customers were invited to take one paper of their choice, free of charge, there is little doubt that far more people would take the *Sun* than one of the left wing papers. Similarly if two concerts were to be broadcast at the same time on prime time TV, one featuring John Coltrane and the other Beyoncé, it is highly likely that the latter would attract hugely more viewers. But recognising an element of truth in an argument does not mean accepting that the argument is true overall. For example, the argument, put endlessly by George Bush and Tony Blair, that the 2003 war on Iraq was justified because Saddam Hussein was a brutal dictator, contained the element of truth that Saddam was a brutal dictator, but overall was a lie for a host of reasons including the fact that Saddam being a dictator was not the reason for the war.

In this case the "only giving them what they want" claim raises at least three important issues: (1) why do people want what they want; (2) why does the media give it to them; and (3) is it true that the media only gives people what they want?

## What shapes our media choices?

What shapes public taste is obviously a huge and complex question which can never be answered exhaustively and certainly not in this small book. However, the key point is that the reason many people prefer the *Sun* or Beyoncé is to do with their social conditioning, not their innate capacities or any in-built right wing bias. Given the right circumstances the mass of ordinary people are perfectly capable of grasping serious political ideas and relating to the best in art and literature: in the Russian Revolution thousands of workers packed in to the Cirque Moderne stadium in Petrograd to hear Lunacharsky, the Commissar for Culture, speak about Greek tragedy; in the Portuguese Revolution of 1974 there was a point when Lenin's great book *The State and Revolution* topped the bestsellers list; militant trade unionists read the *Financial Times* to see what "the other side" is thinking.

By people's social conditioning I mean the totality of their experience from birth onwards: everything from their infant upbringing, through their experience of school to their working and living conditions as adults and to the way in which culture, in its broadest sense, is presented to them.

A huge amount of sociological and educational research demonstrates that educational attainment at every level, from primary school to university, is closely related to and massively affected by social class background. There is a long running debate about which specific aspects of the class experience—income, parental attitudes, peer pressure, institutional and teacher bias, etc—are the most important mechanism in producing this relationship, but the relationship itself is not open to serious doubt. For example, the *Guardian* reported in 2006:

> A study by academics at University College London (UCL) and King's College London has given statistical backbone to the view that the overwhelming factor in how well children do is not what type of school they attend—but social class…
>
> The report, which uses previously unreleased information from the Department for Education and Skills, matches almost 1 million pupils with their individual postcode and exam scores at 11 and 15…
>
> This unprecedented project has revealed that a child's social background is the crucial factor in academic performance, and that a school's success is based not on its teachers, the way it is run, or what type of school it is, but, overwhelmingly, on the class background of its pupils.[22]

And again, in the *Independent* in 2008:

> Children's social class is still the most significant factor in determining their exam success in state schools, the government's head of teacher training acknowledges today.

In an interview with the *Independent*, Graham Holley, the chief executive of the Training and Development Agency, said: "The performance of a school and a child in it is highly linked to social class.

"If you turn the clock back on pupils in school today 15 years and predict their outcomes from where they were born, you can do it".[23]

And it is very obvious why this should be the case. Parental income, which is linked to class, will influence the number of books a child has access to, the availability of space to study in, the opportunity for culturally enriching holidays. Class prejudice, which, though seldom acknowledged, is very widespread (especially at a sub- or semi-conscious level), will influence a school's expectation and assessment of a child's performance. Knowing that working class children tend to end up in working class jobs will influence both parental and pupil attitudes to education. And all of these and many other factors will reinforce each other in such a way that the large majority of children achieve far less than they are capable of, while at the same time probably explaining this in terms of their own incapacity or lack of intelligence. In contrast the upper classes are able to buy a multitude of educational advantages for their children, including so-called public schools and, with the advent of fees, places at the top universities.

This in turn has a major impact on their media and cultural choices. Their "experience" will have conditioned them to feel that certain newspapers, magazines, films, books, museums, concerts and so on are "not for people like them", whereas they will feel more "comfortable" with others, and this is a two-way process—all media products are consciously targeted at specific social groups. To return to the example of the *Sun*, it is owned by the same company and individual (Rupert Murdoch's News Corporation) as the *Times* and has basically the same right wing politics but it is specifically tailored for a working class audience—it is almost written with a working class accent—whereas the *Times* just as strongly signals its middle to upper class allegiance.

The hard facts of working class life—long hours and hard boring work combined with high levels of stress—are another factor. Many people, after an exhausting day at work in the factory or office or coping with kids, simply feel too tired to deal with a newspaper or book or TV programme that demands much attention or effort, and the corporations that supply news and entertainment are on hand to provide just the easy reading/listening/viewing that fits the bill. This is not something that sets working class people apart. Everyone, including professors and PhD students, feels that way some of the time—"I just felt like watching some mindless crap", as people say—but the nature of working class life means working class people, ie most people, feel that way more of the time than do the middle or upper classes.

And here we must bear in mind that radical or challenging ideas always seem more difficult than ideas which reinforce the status quo. Consider the question, "Why do we have a queen?" The various conservative and monarchist answers—because she represents Britain, because it's good for the country, because she attracts tourism, because the monarchy creates stability—require only a phrase, while the real answer involves a history lesson.

However, there is also something much deeper involved. It is what Marx called "alienation". This is a philosophical term which requires some explanation but which relates to people's everyday experience of life under capitalism. Marx set out his theory of alienation in his *Economic and Philosophical Manuscripts* at the very beginning of his development of Marxism, but it remained central to all his subsequent theoretical work. His starting point was that labour, work on nature, is central to what makes us human and to the whole course of human history. It was through labour, the production of the means of subsistence, that human beings differentiated themselves from other animals, and initiated a process of historical development—from foraging to agriculture and industry—as opposed to merely having a natural history. It is through labour on nature that human beings literally shape and make the world they live in, and in the process shape and make themselves. But under capitalism people, especially workers, had lost control of their labour and of the products of their labour. Workers' labour was alienated, ie made over to someone else (the employer) and turned into something alien and damaging to the worker:

> What, then, constitutes the alienation of labour?
>
> First, the fact that labour is external to the worker, ie, it does not belong to his intrinsic nature; that in his work, therefore, he does not affirm himself but denies himself, does not feel content but unhappy, does not develop freely his physical and mental energy but mortifies his body and ruins his mind... He feels at home when he is not working, and when he is working he does not feel at home. His labour is therefore not voluntary, but coerced; it is forced labour... Its alien character emerges clearly in the fact that as soon as no physical or other compulsion exists, labour is shunned like the plague.[24]

Marx argues that the effects of alienated labour extend far beyond our "working life": we are alienated from our own human nature, our ability to consciously shape the world around us; from other people, who we confront as competitors; and from nature and our environment—the very existence of which is now threatened by capitalist production.

How does this general social and personal alienation feed into "what people want" from the media? In the first place it means they are likely to want material that is degraded and damaging, including damaging to themselves. And sure enough they do. There is a big demand for: (a) gratuitous meaningless violence—action movies, comic books, video games and so on; (b) gratuitous meaningless sex—and not just in the pornography industry as such but on mainstream TV (often disguised as "documentary"); and (c) general "freak show" material, presented in a voyeuristic manner. It also means that just as alienation gives rise to religion, in which people create images of god and heaven invested with human aspirations and attributes, so people who are alienated in their labour and from the products of their labour give money and commodities semi-human, semi-magical powers. And huge swathes of the media constantly feed this fetishisation, not only, as we have seen, through game shows and advertising where it is most blatant, but in many other ways such as lifestyle features and product placement.

The overall effect of alienation is that people do not control their world or their lives. They feel powerless and ignored, reduced like Charlie Chaplin in *Modern Times* to mere "appendages of the machine"—even, it should be said, when their material standard of living is quite tolerable. This creates a demand for illusory power and recognition—as in being able to vote for the winner of *The X Factor* or the survival of John Sergeant in *Strictly Come Dancing*, supposedly in "defiance" of the judges, or identifying with "ordinary people" like Susan Boyle or Chantelle who become super-celebrities for a day or so. Clearly this is a demand the media is more than happy to meet.

Alienation also generates a certain resistance, even hostility, to material—artistic or political—that actually challenges alienation. Prisoners who have served long sentences often become "institutionalised" and cannot cope with life outside jail. Similarly many people who accept and internalise their alienation, who have reconciled themselves to powerlessness and adopted compliance with the status quo as a life strategy, find media output that points out or analyses their alienation or calls on them to resist it or shows their potential power—say a Billie Holiday song or a play by Pinter or Brecht or a Ken Loach film—very painful and unwelcome. Once again the media is happy to oblige by keeping the dissemination of such awkward material to a minimum.

## A spoonful of sugar...

If the media is giving people what they want we have to ask not only why they want it but also why the media gives it to them. The question is very simple and the answer quite obvious, but it matters.

On the first page of *Capital* Marx points out, "A commodity is, in the first place, an object outside us, a thing that by its properties satisfies human wants of some sort or another".[25] If people did not want any particular commodity, if it had no "use value", as Marx calls it, the capitalist would not be able to sell it. But, as Marx also points out, this does not mean that the capitalist sells commodities in order to satisfy people's wants or needs; on the contrary the capitalist sells commodities in order to make a profit, and if he/she ceases to make a profit, stops selling them and halts production. Nor does the fact that people need or want something mean, in a capitalist economy, that it will be produced or that they will get it. There are many millions of people in the world who desperately need and want food but since they are poor it is not profitable to supply them with it and they starve. There is a need and demand for affordable housing, and also a demand for luxury hotels, but if it is more profitable to meet the demand for luxury hotels that is what will tend to get built.

This has a number of implications for the output of the media, almost all of which takes the form of commodities. In the first place it means that out of the numerous and varied wants and demands in society, the capitalists (and state appointees) who control 99 percent of the mass media can decide which demands to meet and which to ignore. For example, if there is a demand among the public for accessible and accurate news of what is happening in the world it is possible to respond to that demand by providing accessible news but not worrying about whether or not it is accurate (as in any tabloid newspaper). Alternatively it is possible to provide relatively serious news coverage but packaged in such a way as to make it inaccessible to a popular audience (as in the *Financial Times*).

Another option is to offer people something they really want—entertainment, comedy, escapism, etc—but laced with something else they didn't want and didn't bargain for. This, of course, is the strategy of the drug dealer, and I include the tobacco companies in this. But it is also very much how the *Sun* works. *Sun* readers undoubtedly want a light-hearted, punchy, easily readable take on the world—they may well also want a paper that panders to some of their prejudices—but do they want one that mixes in with all these elements systematic propaganda in favour of whichever political party the proprietor, Rupert Murdoch, is on side with at the time?

At the same time, where Murdoch is concerned, this is not just a question of the immediate sales figures of the *Sun*. He is head of a vast global corporation with global concerns and interests, and also has a strongly developed political or class instinct. So big decisions as to the editorial policy of the *Sun* reflect all these things including the need to avoid stories which would give comfort to the left, ie in any way challenge the economic system, capitalism, which Murdoch supports and which underwrites the profits of News Corporation.

Just how directly, though covertly, political Murdoch is needs emphasising. He has had personal meetings with every US president since Harry Truman. In 2008 he met with Barack Obama at the Waldorf Astoria Hotel in New York. According to Michael Wolff (Murdoch's biographer) writing in *Vanity Fair*:

> Murdoch, for his part, had a simple thought to share with Obama. He had known possibly as many heads of state as anyone living today…and this is what he understood: nobody got much time to make an impression. Leadership was about what you did in the first six months.
>
> Then, after he said his piece, Murdoch switched places and let his special guest, Roger Ailes [President of Fox News], sit knee to knee with Obama.
>
> Obama lit into Ailes. He said that he didn't want to waste his time talking to Ailes if Fox was just going to continue to abuse him and his wife, that Fox had relentlessly portrayed him as suspicious, foreign, fearsome—just short of a terrorist.
>
> Ailes, unruffled, said it might not have been this way if Obama had more willingly come on the air instead of so often giving Fox the back of his hand.
>
> A tentative truce, which may or may not have vast historical significance, was at that moment agreed upon.[26]

In the 1980s he was closely linked to Margaret Thatcher and all his papers backed her strongly. Support for the Tories continued under Major and the *Sun*, notoriously, claimed credit for winning Major the 1992 election ("It's The *Sun* Wot Won It" was the headline). Then Murdoch shifted his allegiance to Tony Blair, after Blair flew to Australia for a personal meeting. The terms of the deal would seem to have been that Murdoch would back Blair, who was likely to win anyway, in return for Labour dropping its plans to legislate against foreign ownership (ie Murdoch's ownership) of British media. But, of course, Blair's right wing, neoliberal, pro-American stance would also have appealed to Murdoch. In August 2008 David Cameron travelled (on free flights, courtesy of Murdoch's son-in-law, Matthew Freud) to meet Murdoch on his yacht. Shortly thereafter Murdoch and his papers switched back to supporting the Tories, and former *News of the World* editor Andy Coulson served as Cameron's communications director until the recent phone hacking scandal.

How Rupert Murdoch operates with the *Sun* and his other popular titles, including of course the *News of the World* until July 2011, is only the most obvious example of how a great deal of the media works—right wing, pro-capitalist politics wrapped in a sugar coating of sport, sex and celebrity scandal. Thus taken as a whole the media "excuse" that it only gives people what they want turns out to be radically false. It is worth adding, however, that a media, such as exists in the so-called "Western democracies", which mixes fact and fiction, information and omission, propaganda and entertainment, is likely to be more believed and more effective for the system than a media such as in Stalinist Russia and Eastern Europe that merely spouts state propaganda and the party line. As Mary Poppins put it, "A spoonful of sugar helps the medicine go down!"

# 4. How powerful are the media?

This question can be posed in two ways: how powerful are the media in relation to other centres of power in our society (eg the government, the state, big business as a whole) and how much power does the media have over the thinking of the mass of ordinary people? I shall consider each in turn.

## The media and the ruling class

When we see Tony Blair travelling to the other side of the world to go cap in hand to Rupert Murdoch or politicians worrying how a policy will play with the *Daily Mail*, it is easy to think of the media as "all powerful". At a recent meeting in London during the Murdoch phone hacking scandal Tony Benn described Murdoch as "probably the most powerful man in the world". Also during the unravelling of that scandal I was sent a video in which a certain Gordon Duff stated, "Murdoch is now admitted to have controlled the political systems in Britain and America for two decades. He has had the power to choose national leaders, make policy, pass laws at will". These sources are not of equal value. Tony Benn is a veteran and hugely respected left winger, Gordon Duff is a crazy conspiracy theorist with a tinge of anti-Semitism, but they both illustrate a widely held view—one which I contest.

Clearly the media as a whole are a powerful force in the world and equally clearly some of the biggest media corporations—Murdoch's News Corporation and Berlusconi's empire—are major economic and political players. However, it is easy, as we see in the quote from

Duff above, to mistakenly exaggerate this power and to see either the media overall or particular media moguls as rulers of the world. Indeed the recent phone hacking scandal showed precisely this. If Murdoch was really the most powerful man in the world or really controlled the political systems in Britain and America he would not have been forced to close the *News of the World*, get rid of his right hand man, Les Hinton, and key subordinate, Rebekah Brooks or fly to Britain to testify, humbly, before a parliamentary committee. Similarly Silvio Berlusconi, despite being Italy's prime minister and owner of three TV stations, has faced numerous charges and challenges in the Italian courts over bribery and corruption. The fact that he has, so far, survived all these is a testimony to his power, but if he were all powerful, even in Italy never mind the world, he would not have had to face them at all.

In order to estimate both the extent and limits of media power we need to understand in general how power works in capitalist society. The best way to do this is to go back to what Marx has to say about the foundations of political power. Marx begins by noting "that man must be in a position to live in order to be able to 'make history'. But life involves before everything else eating and drinking, a habitation, clothing and many other things".[27] From this starting point he goes on to say:

> In the social production of their existence, men inevitably enter into definite relations, which are independent of their will, namely relations of production appropriate to a given stage in the development of their material forces of production. The totality of these relations of production constitutes the economic structure of society, the real foundation, on which arises a legal and political superstructure and to which correspond definite forms of social consciousness. The mode of production of material life conditions the general process

of social, political and intellectual life.[28]

Political power, therefore, rests ultimately on economic power. This is not a simple mechanical relationship, but the economy is fundamental. As Engels put it:

Political, juridical, philosophical, religious, literary, artistic, etc, development is based on economic development. But all these react upon one another and also upon the economic base. It is not that the economic position is the cause and alone active, while everything else only has a passive effect. There is, rather, interaction on the basis of the economic necessity, which ultimately always asserts itself.[29]

For Marx societies in general are dominated by the social class which owns and controls the major means of production, and modern society is dominated by the bourgeoisie, "the class of modern capitalists, owners of the means of social production and employers of wage labour", as they are defined in *The Communist Manifesto*. The capitalist class are what Marx calls the ruling class. They are like "hostile brothers" in that they compete with one another to make profits but have a common interest in holding down the working class and preserving the system. To manage the general affairs of society in its interests, the capitalist class has created and uses the apparatus of the state. "The executive of the modern state", says Marx in the *Manifesto*, "is but a committee for managing the common affairs of the whole bourgeoisie." The state has both to overcome the divisions between capitalists and to defend capitalism against any threats from below.

How does the media fit into this? First, as we know, it is overwhelmingly owned and controlled by big corporations such as Time Warner, Disney, Organizachoes Globo (Brazil), Nippon Television Network Corporation (Japan), Bouygues S A (France) and News Corporation, all of whose owners are part of the ruling class. And where it is publicly owned it is controlled by states which represent the collective interests of capital.

However, the media is by no means the dominant part of the ruling class. Let us start by considering this purely economically. There are a number of ways of measuring the size of companies—by revenues, profits, assets, employees, etc—and a number of lists of the world's top companies. But by any criteria and on all the lists the largest media corporations are tiny by comparison with the biggest international companies. Wikipedia lists 200 companies ranked by revenues, with Wal-Mart ($421bn) top, followed by ExxonMobil ($370bn) and Royal Dutch Shell ($368bn).[30] On this list no media company makes the top 200. The CNN Fortune Global 500 list, which also ranks by revenues, puts Wal-Mart ($421bn), Royal Dutch Shell ($378bn) and Exxon Mobil ($354bn) in the top three spots, while the highest ranked media company, Walt Disney ($38bn), comes in at 226, followed by News Corp ($32.7bn) at 284 and Time Warner ($26.8bn) at 363. If the field is restricted to the US, Fortune 500 places Walt Disney at 65, News Corp at 83 and Time Warner at 95.[31] The *Financial Times* Global 500 ranks by "market value" and on this list the media companies come higher: Walt Disney ($81bn) is at 75, News Corp ($47bn) is at 171, and Time Warner ($39bn) at 211. But out of the whole 500 there are only 12 media companies listed compared to 76 oil and gas companies and 75 banks.[32] A combination of the Wikipedia and the *Financial Times* lists also enables us to compare companies in terms of numbers of employees. Disney employs 149,000, News Corp 51,000 and Time Warner 31,000 compared to Wal-Mart's 2,150,000, Tesco's 492,000, Siemens 405,000, Volkswagen's 329,000 and HSBC's 302,000.

This relative lack of size (of course they are giants compared to small or average sized businesses) has real effects in terms of the influence of the media companies within the ruling class. They are not, for example, generally in the category of companies that are "too big to be allowed to fail". When Murdoch closed the *News of the World* the main consequences were political and ideological rather than economic (except for the workers who lost their jobs). Also media companies are not by and large able to blackmail governments by threatening to relocate. Murdoch cannot move Fox News or the *Sun* to Indonesia or the *Wall Street Journal* to the Mexican border.

What then of the political power of the media? Here it is necessary to distinguish between individual politicians, political parties, governments and states. Clearly the media, especially if they act in concert, have the power on occasion to break (or significantly boost) individual politicians. But this usually involves the politician being caught out in some serious misdemeanour like Nixon over Watergate—the media did their best to break Tony Benn and Ken Livingstone in the 1980s and most certainly damaged them, but they did not destroy them. Nor can I think of an instance of a media campaign, in and of itself, bringing down a government (unlike people power and popular uprisings which have brought down many governments from that of Louis XVI to that of Hosni Mubarak). Of course a government in severe crisis may be helped or hindered by the nature of its media coverage and the media may exercise a significant influence in elections (this is discussed further in the next section), which is why the leaders of political parties go to some lengths to court the media, but in these situations the attitude of the media is only one factor among many (such as the state of the economy and the popularity of the party's policies).

Moreover politicians and governments are only one part of the state. Although nominally they run the various state apparatuses (armed forces, judiciary, civil service, police, etc) in practice it tends to be the other way round. And one thing we can say for sure is that the media is far more the servant than it is the master of the state taken as a whole—precisely because the state represents the general interests of the capitalist class.

Most of the time the different wings of the ruling class—economic, political, judicial, etc—though nominally independent of each other, in fact collaborate behind the scenes and mind each other's backs. The revelations in the Murdoch scandal provided a number of snapshots of such collaboration: the close links between the Cameron government, the Murdoch empire and the Metropolitan Police. But the scandal also shows that when things go wrong and there is a crisis, there is also a real pecking order and hierarchy of power and the media do not stand at the top of it.

As we have seen, the media performs for the capitalist class and the capitalist state the very important service of systematic legitimation, of continually reinforcing the naturalness and inevitability of their rule, and this allows it to punch well above its strict economic weight. News Corp stands at 171 in the *Financial Times* list cited above but clearly it is much more powerful and politically important than Teva Pharmaceuticals and Metlife that stand at 169 and 170 respectively. If, however, the behaviour of a section of the media—and this was the case, in different ways, with both the BBC and the dossier and with the Murdoch scandal—starts to undermine that legitimacy, then the state, as guardian of the overall interests of the capitalist class, intervenes to rein it in.

## How much do they control us?

We are surrounded by the media. Almost everyone owns at least one television, and TV reaches 44 million people a day, 54 million a week for an average of 26 hours a week.[33] Newspaper readership remains high—the *Sun* sells 3 million copies a day, the *Daily Mail* over 2 million and the *Daily Mirror* 1.2 million.[34] We all hear on a daily basis people talking about what they saw on telly or read in the paper, often repeating what they have seen or read uncritically.

In 1845, before any of the modern mass media had come into existence (when the top selling paper was the *Illustrated London News* at about 80,000 a week), Karl Marx wrote in *The German Ideology* that:

> The ideas of the ruling class are in every epoch the ruling ideas, ie the class which is the ruling material force of society, is at the same time its ruling intellectual force. The class which has the means of material production at its disposal, has control at the same time over the means of mental production, so that thereby, generally speaking, the ideas of those who lack the means of mental production are subject to it.[35]

The huge influence of the media today is simply the main contemporary form of this general truth about the ruling classes' ideological dominance or hegemony, as it is often called. In Marx's day, and for many centuries before, the church was the main instrument of ideological rule. Today the TV presenter has largely replaced the priest—though the priest is still there and the education system, from infant school to university, is also important.

But even for Marx himself the proposition that "the class which is the ruling material force of society is at the same time its ruling intellectual force" cannot be the whole story or it would have invalidated his whole life's work, which was based on the belief that the working class could free itself from the ruling ideas. "The proletarian movement", he wrote in *The Communist Manifesto*, "is the *self-conscious*, independent movement of the immense majority, in the interest of the immense majority" (my emphasis—JM).

So the notion that we are all totally brainwashed by the media falls at the first hurdle, for if we were I could not have written this booklet and you, the reader, would not be reading it, and clearly you and I are not the only ones to have "escaped". More importantly there is lots of evidence that sometimes, at least, large numbers of people do not accept the interpretations of the world being beamed at them via the media. In the introduction I cited the example of the mass opposition to the Iraq war in 2003 despite the media's overwhelming support for it (of the main newspapers only the *Daily Mirror* was against, and only until the war started). 2011 provided an even more vivid and dramatic example— the Egyptian Revolution. It goes without saying that under the Mubarak dictatorship the media, both in Egypt and internationally, was not pro-revolution; indeed it was in the main not even mildly critical. Yet something in the region of 15 million people took part in the final anti-Mubarak mobilisations of 10 to 11 February,[36] and post-revolution opinion polls show large majorities in favour of it. The poll results from the Washington-based Pew Global Attitudes Project showed that two thirds of Egyptians questioned are optimistic about the future, and an overwhelming number said they are glad former President Hosni Mubarak is gone.[37]

At a more mundane level there is a lot of evidence on the degree of correspondence between newspapers' political allegiance and their readers' actual voting behaviour.

| *Daily Express* | 1992 | 1997 | 2001 | 2005 | 2010 |
|---|---|---|---|---|---|
| | % | % | % | % | % |
| Estimated turnout | | | 63 | 69 | 67 |
| Conservative | 68 | 49 | 43 | 48 | 53 |
| Labour | 15 | 29 | 33 | 28 | 19 |
| Liberal Democrat | 15 | 16 | 19 | 18 | 18 |
| Others | 2 | 6 | 5 | 6 | 10 |
| Con lead | +53 | +20 | +10 | +20 | +34 |
| Con-Lab swing election-to-election | | +16.5 | +5.0 | -5.0 | -7.0 |

| Daily Mail | 1992 | 1997 | 2001 | 2005 | 2010 |
|---|---|---|---|---|---|
| | % | % | % | % | % |
| Estimated turnout | | | 65 | 69 | 73 |
| Conservative | 65 | 49 | 55 | 57 | 59 |
| Labour | 14 | 29 | 24 | 22 | 16 |
| Liberal Democrat | 18 | 14 | 17 | 14 | 16 |
| Others | 3 | 8 | 4 | 7 | 9 |
| Con lead | +51 | +20 | +31 | +35 | +43 |
| Con-Lab swing election-to-election | | +15.5 | -5.5 | -2.0 | -4.0 |

| Daily Mirror | 1992 | 1997 | 2001 | 2005 | 2010 |
|---|---|---|---|---|---|
| | % | % | % | % | % |
| Estimated turnout | | | 62 | 63 | 68 |
| Conservative | 20 | 14 | 11 | 11 | 16 |
| Labour | 63 | 72 | 71 | 67 | 59 |
| Liberal Democrat | 14 | 11 | 13 | 17 | 17 |
| Others | 3 | 3 | 5 | 5 | 8 |
| Con lead | -43 | -58 | -60 | -56 | -43 |
| Con-Lab swing election-to-election | | +7.5 | +1.0 | -2.0 | -6.5 |

| Daily Record | 1992 | 1997 | 2001 | 2005 | 2010 |
|---|---|---|---|---|---|
| | % | % | % | % | % |
| Estimated turnout | | | 57 | 59 | 65 |
| Conservative | 14 | 12 | 8 | 7 | 12 |
| Labour | 55 | 57 | 59 | 55 | 65 |
| Liberal Democrat | 7 | 10 | 10 | 16 | 6 |
| Others | 24 | 21 | 23 | 22 | 17 |
| Con lead | -41 | -45 | -51 | -48 | -53 |
| Con-Lab swing election-to-election | | +2.0 | +3.0 | -1.5 | +2.5 |

| *Daily Telegraph* | 1992 | 1997 | 2001 | 2005 | 2010 |
|---|---|---|---|---|---|
| | % | % | % | % | % |
| Estimated turnout | | | 71 | 77 | 81 |
| Conservative | 72 | 57 | 65 | 65 | 70 |
| Labour | 11 | 20 | 16 | 13 | 7 |
| Liberal Democrat | 16 | 17 | 14 | 17 | 18 |
| Others | 1 | 6 | 5 | 5 | 5 |
| Con lead | +61 | +37 | +49 | +52 | +63 |
| Con-Lab swing election-to-election | | +12.0 | -6.0 | -1.5 | -5.5 |

| *Financial Times* | 1992 | 1997 | 2001 | 2005 | 2010 |
|---|---|---|---|---|---|
| | % | % | % | % | % |
| Estimated turnout | | | 64 | 65 | * |
| Conservative | 65 | 48 | 48 | 47 | |
| Labour | 17 | 29 | 30 | 29 | |
| Liberal Democrat | 16 | 19 | 21 | 21 | |
| Others | 2 | 4 | 1 | 3 | |
| Con lead | +48 | +19 | +18 | +18 | |
| Con-Lab swing election-to-election | | +14.5 | +0.5 | 0.0 | |

| *Guardian* | 1992 | 1997 | 2001 | 2005 | 2010 |
|---|---|---|---|---|---|
| | % | % | % | % | % |
| Estimated turnout | | | 68 | 73 | 78 |
| Conservative | 15 | 8 | 6 | 7 | 9 |
| Labour | 55 | 67 | 52 | 43 | 46 |
| Liberal Democrat | 25 | 22 | 34 | 41 | 37 |
| Others | 5 | 3 | 8 | 9 | 8 |
| Con lead | -40 | -59 | -46 | -36 | -37 |
| Con-Lab swing election-to-election | | +9.5 | -6.5 | -5.0 | +0.5 |

---

\* Sample too small to offer a robust measurement.

| *Independent* | 1992 | 1997 | 2001 | 2005 | 2010 |
|---|---|---|---|---|---|
| | % | % | % | % | % |
| Estimated turnout | | | 69 | 76 | 79 |
| Conservative | 25 | 16 | 12 | 13 | 14 |
| Labour | 37 | 47 | 38 | 34 | 32 |
| Liberal Democrat | 35 | 30 | 44 | 44 | 44 |
| Others | 3 | 7 | 6 | 9 | 10 |
| Con lead | -12 | -31 | -26 | -21 | -18 |
| Con-Lab swing election-to-election | | +9.5 | -2.5 | -2.5 | -1.5 |

| *Daily Star* | 1992 | 1997 | 2001 | 2005 | 2010 |
|---|---|---|---|---|---|
| | % | % | % | % | % |
| Estimated turnout | | | 48 | 46 | 43 |
| Conservative | 32 | 17 | 21 | 21 | 22 |
| Labour | 53 | 66 | 56 | 54 | 35 |
| Liberal Democrat | 12 | 12 | 17 | 15 | 20 |
| Others | 3 | 5 | 6 | 10 | 23 |
| Con lead | -21 | -49 | -35 | -33 | -13 |
| Con-Lab swing election-to-election | | +14.0 | -7.0 | -1.0 | -10.0 |

| *Sun* | 1992 | 1997 | 2001 | 2005 | 2010 |
|---|---|---|---|---|---|
| | % | % | % | % | % |
| Estimated turnout | | | 50 | 52 | 57 |
| Conservative | 45 | 30 | 29 | 33 | 43 |
| Labour | 36 | 52 | 52 | 45 | 28 |
| Liberal Democrat | 15 | 12 | 11 | 12 | 18 |
| Others | 4 | 6 | 8 | 10 | 11 |
| Con lead | +9 | -22 | -23 | -12 | +15 |
| Con-Lab swing election-to-election | | +15.5 | +0.5 | -5.5 | -13.5 |

| *Times* | 1992 | 1997 | 2001 | 2005 | 2010 |
|---|---|---|---|---|---|
| | % | % | % | % | % |
| Estimated turnout | | | 66 | 71 | 80 |
| Conservative | 64 | 42 | 40 | 38 | 49 |
| Labour | 15 | 28 | 28 | 27 | 22 |
| Liberal Democrat | 19 | 25 | 26 | 28 | 24 |
| Others | 2 | 5 | 6 | 7 | 5 |
| Con lead | +49 | +14 | +12 | +11 | +27 |
| Con-Lab swing election-to-election | | +17.5 | +1.0 | +0.5 | -8.0 |

Source: Ipsos MORI General Election aggregates.
http://www.ipsos-mori.com/researchpublications/researcharchive/
2476/Voting-by-Newspaper-Readership-19922010.aspx?view=wide

These figures show a number of things. First that a majority of the readers of the very clearly and consistently right wing papers, ie *Daily Express*, *Daily Mail* and *Daily Telegraph*, voted Conservative in 2010 and have pretty much always done so. But this may be at least as much, and probably more, because Conservative voters choose to read those papers as because they are influenced to vote that way by the paper. However, even in the cases of the *Mail* and the *Express*, which are pretty rabid, a significant minority votes Labour or Liberal Democrat—in the case of the *Express* 37 percent in 2010 and 45 percent in the Labour landslide year of 1997, and in the case of the *Mail* 32 percent in 2010 and 43 percent in 1997. Even the "Torygraph" shared this fate to some extent, with 25 percent in 2010 and 37 percent in 1997. This indicates that even the readers of these very right wing papers were affected by what might be called the "political mood" in the country.

Also revealing is the comparison between the *Times* and the *Sun*. Both are owned by News Corp and Rupert Murdoch and so toe fundamentally the same political line—right of centre in general, pro-Tory in 2010—though the *Sun* is naturally much more populist. However, in 2010 22 percent of *Times* readers voted Labour (plus 24 percent Lib Dem), while 28 percent of *Sun* readers voted Labour, plus 18 percent Lib Dem, which together with "Others" meant 57 percent did not vote the way their paper suggested. The difference between the figures for the *Times* and the *Sun* is almost certainly to do with average social class position of the readers. We should note that in 1997 and 2001 when the *Sun* supported Blair and New Labour, so too did 52 percent of its readers, which could imply significant influence but may also have been a case of the paper following its readers to some extent.

The case of the *Daily Star* is also interesting. It is the most "down market" and "trashy" of the tabloids with the least coverage of political news and lowest circulation (suggesting most working class people want something better). Its proprietor is Richard Desmond who also owns the *Daily Express* (which has a long tradition of featuring anti-immigrant, anti-asylum seeker stories). In February 2011 the *Star* moved further to the right than any other national newspaper and carried a front page article which came close to endorsing the racist and fascist English Defence League and ended with the highly doubtful claim that, "In the *Daily Star* phone poll yesterday, 98 percent of readers said they agreed with the EDL's policies".[38] Yet the IPSOS figures above show that among the minority of *Star* readers who vote at all, Labour has consistently polled highest and did so in 2010, although its vote had shrunk to 35 percent and "others", which might include the BNP (closely related to the EDL), had risen to 23 percent.

Taken as a whole the figures demonstrate clearly that newspapers do not in any simple way control the political thinking of their readers. They do exercise some influence but that influence is modified and to a considerable extent counteracted by their class position and allegiance. It is the fact that, despite the best efforts of Tony Blair, Labour is still widely perceived as the party of the working class that explains why a significant proportion of the readers of right wing tabloids consistently vote Labour and why, where politics and class reinforce each other as in the Labour-supporting *Daily Mirror*, the Labour vote is massive—72 percent in 1997 and 59 percent in 2010.

This in turn points to a wider generalisation. The media is neither all powerful nor impotent. The political ideas of the mass of people are shaped by many factors, the two most important of which are the worldview handed down to them from the ruling class (via the media, the education system, politicians, the churches, etc—probably in that order of significance) and their own social experience. Generally speaking these two forces tend to pull in opposite directions and produce what Antonio Gramsci called "contradictory consciousness"—they believe in the profit motive in the abstract but think their boss is a greedy bastard, they are patriotic and "believe in the country" but in practice want to emigrate, and so on.

From this it follows that media influence will vary according to issues and circumstances. It will tend to be weakest when dealing with matters of direct personal experience and strongest when dealing with events or processes of which people don't or can't have experience.

Take for example the question of mass unemployment. Far too many people have personal experience of unemployment, directly or through relations and friends, to spin it as a good thing, even though there are definitely times when the ruling class think it is "a price well worth paying", as Tory chancellor of the exchequer Norman Lamont put it in 1991. Therefore all public figures, and the media, have no choice but to treat unemployment as a misfortune, even when they are actually sacking large numbers of people or pursuing economic policies that will inevitably increase it. The underlying causes of unemployment are a different matter, however. These are frequently not directly experienced but hidden in the labyrinthine entrails of the capitalist economy. So when it comes to apportioning blame for unemployment the media and politicians have much more room for manoeuvre and can target immigrants, blacks, asylum seekers or whoever is the scapegoat on hand.

In contrast very few (British) people have experience of being an asylum seeker; indeed few people even get to know them. Consequently it is possible to make up endless stories of asylum seekers on £500 a week, living the life of Riley at "our" expense in posh hotels or jumping to the front of the housing queue while simultaneously "taking our jobs"— and, crucially, have them believed by considerable numbers of people. The technique of highlighting an isolated incident as if it were typical, which if done on a regular basis creates a completely false impression, is a particular favourite.

Another illustration of the same point is the difference in style and tone between local and national papers. Local papers are much less inclined than the nationals to attack, humiliate and invade the privacy of members of their community. This is because the victimised individuals are likely to be known to many of their readers, whereas with the nationals they will be known only to an infinitesimal proportion, and so can be attacked with relative impunity.

When the issue is outside of people's direct experience the extent to which they have access to alternative sources of information will make a considerable difference. For example individuals who read a single report, or a series of reports saying the same thing, about Afghanistan are more likely to believe what they are told than if they are aware that there are different accounts and different points of view. And they are much more likely to have such access if they are members of groups or organisations or communities that share an "oppositional" view. W L Miller's study of the media in the 1987 general election concluded:

The media set the agenda for only a part of their audience: those highly reliant on a particular news source, those low in political involvement and information, and those who are relatively inattentive to politics generally—in short, those who are marginal to politics.[39]

Similarly David Morley's report on the way different groups interpreted one edition of BBC news and current affairs programme *Nationwide* argued:

It is the [trade union] shop stewards that spontaneously produce by far the most articulate, fully oppositional reading of the programme. They reject the programme's attempt to tell us what "our grouse" is and its attempt to construct a national "we". This group fulfils the criteria of an oppositional reading in the precise sense that it redefines the issues which the programme presents. Its members are critical of what they see as significant absences in the discussion of economics.[40]

All of this has very important implications for the circumstances in which the influence of the capitalist media would be at its weakest: it would be when large masses of the population are drawn into direct action or struggle in mass demonstrations and/or strikes. In these conditions millions of people's direct experience, their own actions, would be the news story. If the media refused to report the struggle they would notice it and draw conclusions; likewise if the media tried to distort or misrepresent the issues or conduct of the protesters or strikers. The masses in struggle would also necessarily be part of groups, networks and organisations that would provide alternative information and generate and support oppositional views.

Here it is useful to note Leon Trotsky's definition of a revolution:

The most indubitable feature of a revolution is the direct

interference of the masses in historical events. In ordinary times the state, be it monarchical or democratic, elevates itself above the nation, and history is made by specialists in that line of business—kings, ministers, bureaucrats, parliamentarians, journalists. But at those crucial moments when the old order becomes no longer endurable to the masses, they break over the barriers excluding them from the political arena, sweep aside their traditional representatives, and create by their own interference the initial groundwork for a new regime.[41]

It is useful to observe how this argument was confirmed by the experience of the Egyptian Revolution in January/February 2011. Whenever violence breaks out on a demonstration, whenever people fight the police the normal practice for the entire capitalist media is to blame the demonstrators and denounce them bitterly. This was what happened after the Grosvenor Square anti Vietnam War demonstration in 1968, after the Poll Tax Riot in 1989, after the Anti Nazi League confrontation with the police at Welling in 1994, and the student demonstrations in November 2010, and on many other occasions. The great demonstrations in Egypt were far more violent than any of these skirmishes—over 800 people were killed and the headquarters of Mubarak's National Democratic Party and virtually every police station in Cairo were set on fire. And yet now the media consensus in Egypt and internationally is that the demonstrators were "peaceful" and the police and pro-Mubarak supporters were violent. In a fundamental sense this is true, but the point is that the vast participation of the people, the fact that literally millions were involved, made it impossible to tell it any other way.

To summarise: the mass media is very influential, especially when most people are passive, but it is by no means all powerful. Its influence fluctuates depending on the issues involved and how they relate to people's experience. Its influence is at its weakest when there is mass resistance.

# 5. Combating the media

It is clear from everything written in this booklet so far that anyone wanting to see serious social change needs a strategy for dealing with the media. In this chapter I want to look at five elements in such a strategy: (a) combating the media in our heads; (b) using the capitalist media; (c) Facebook, Twitter and all that; (d) mass action; and (e) political organisation. I will discuss these in order but they are intended to be complementary, not alternatives. They all need to be pursued more or less all of the time with the emphasis varying depending on circumstances.

But I want to start by ruling out three options: first that it is possible to achieve change while simply collaborating with the media as it is and on its own terms; second that the media can be substantially reformed or neutralised by parliamentary legislation; third that we can simply reject it wholesale, stop reading the papers and switch off the TV.

If you are a mainstream professional politician and you want to advance your career, becoming "media savvy", learning how to conduct yourself in a Paxman interview or on *Question Time*, getting focus group advice to find out what soundbites and which hairstyles go down well on the *Six O'Clock News*, knowing how to get stories planted in the papers, having the telephone numbers of newspaper editors or better still going to dinner with them, may all be very useful indeed. If you are involved in radical campaigning—a trade unionist or student activist, fighting cuts, or defending a hospital or fighting racism or war—some of these skills may also come in handy from time to time, though you will get much less opportunity to use them, especially going to dinner with the editor of the *Daily Mail*.

But the notion that such an approach offers a strategy or method of changing either the media or society is completely false. The influence that you as an individual or a radical campaign can have on the media may be useful in certain instances but it cannot change or seriously modify its thoroughly pro-capitalist and generally right wing character. Taken too far, or pursued uncritically, this approach is likely to lead to subservience to the media—the internalisation and adoption of its norms and values—and therefore the weakening or abandonment of the campaign or organisation's radical aims.

New Labour's media strategy is an extreme example. It was based around the combination of low level bullying of journalists (particularly by Blair's press secretary, Alastair Campbell) and high level cringing by Blair himself with Rupert Murdoch and others. This worked pretty well in terms of securing favourable media coverage and thus helping Blair win elections, but the condition of the deal was, and was always going to be, that Labour ditched any policies in any way threatening to capitalism. The same logic applies, on a smaller scale, to any campaign. Consider, for example, that you are a trade unionist representing a group of workers with a grievance, say a threatened pay cut. Media skills may well be useful but if that becomes the main strategy it will undermine the workers' struggle because the capitalist media are virtually always opposed to strikes or militant workers' action, no matter how telegenic or media savvy the union official may be.

From time to time, and especially when there is a scandal about media behaviour, there are vociferous calls for new laws to control media behaviour, restrict infringement of privacy, etc. Press spokespeople are then invariably wheeled out to object that such laws would only serve to limit press freedom and protect dirty dealing politicians from investigative journalism. The problem in these cases is basically that both sides are telling the truth about the other but lying about themselves. In other words the media frequently behave appallingly, in ways that should be stopped, but laws to try to achieve such ends would probably be used to hinder or block investigative journalism and protect politicians and others in high places. But either way the main problem would not be solved. No law enacted by parliament is going to challenge or be able to challenge the fundamental capitalist control and therefore capitalist bias of the vast bulk of the media in a capitalist society.

Refusal to engage with the media is also not viable if the aim is social change. As we have seen the art of propaganda does not consist of simply lying about the world. It consists of mixing fact and fiction, of combining information and interpretation in such a way as the viewer or reader fails to discern which is which. Much of the information in even the trashiest tabloid is actually true: the date on the paper is true; the TV listings are accurate; the sports results are correct and so on. If the *Sun* reports that the queen has died or the prime minister has resigned that will be true—the lie would too easily exposed. TV News, or broadsheet newspapers like the *Financial Times* or the *Guardian* contain huge amounts of information about the world which is both true and useful to know. No serious attempt to change the world, or even to present a different account of it, can do without this information. Nor can any "alternative", "independent" or radical sources match the financial, technical and political resources of the big corporations and state broadcasting companies until such time as the social order is changed. Therefore there is no choice but to make use of the capitalist media at the same time as struggling against it, in the same way that there is no viable choice but to shop at capitalist stores until such time as capitalism is overthrown.

## Combating the media in our heads

"My personal feeling is that citizens of the democratic soci-eties should undertake a course of intellectual self-defence to protect themselves from manipulation and control" (Noam Chomsky).[42] What we all need to do is to learn to read the media against the grain: to be able to judge when it is likely to be telling the truth and when it is likely to be lying; to be able to separate fact from opinion; to be aware of where the opinion is coming from, ie what prejudices, stances and interests they represent; to grasp why the par-ticular selection of news in a particular paper or news bul-letin has been constructed in the way it has, and what is likely to have been left out.

Part of this is a matter of being aware of particular tricks the media regularly uses. For example, the way views which are actually those of the programme or newspaper are pro-jected on to the public in general or particular individuals and then reported as fact: "A storm broke out yesterday about X", or, "There was outrage in Westminster last night over Y." In many cases there is no "storm" or "outrage" at all among the public, especially before the incident or issue is even reported, and often also after it has been reported—rather the "storm" has just been made up by the reporter. And when the "storm" is exemplified or instanced by quotes from politicians or public figures, it is necessary to be aware that such people have most likely been specifically rung up by the media for that purpose. Indeed some politicians get themselves a reputation for "giving good quotes".

We also need to be aware of the loaded way the media uses language: the way strike days are always "lost" rather than "gained" and invariably cause "disruption" or "incon-venience" to "the public" with strikers never being regarded as "members of the public". It is very important to decode the use of "extremist" and "moderate". If you hear or read a report of any conflict anywhere in the world, especially somewhere you know nothing about—Outer Mongolia or Paraguay—and one faction, party or leader is described as "moderate" while the other is said to be "extremist" you know instantly (a) which side our government is on and (b) which side *you* are supposed to be on. It works the same if it is "moderates" or "extremists" in the trade unions.

But if "extremist" is linked to Muslim it shifts. An extremist trade unionist probably means a socialist or communist (before I retired I was a trade union extremist, ie a socialist member of the University and College Union). An "extremist Muslim", however, signifies a terrorist—a planter of bombs, etc—except that you can call someone an extremist without any proof or even evidence that they actually are a terrorist. Then again there is the way extremist Muslim has morphed into "radical" Muslim. Radical, when linked to non-Muslims, meant something akin to left wing, liberal or socialist; the British "radical" tradition might stretch from Tom Paine through Shelley and William Morris to George Orwell and Tony Benn—certainly a significant strand in British history and political life, perhaps something to be proud of. But in media discourse it is perfectly normal to talk about preventing Muslims from "radicalising", because radical now also signifies terrorist, without the shift in meaning ever being acknowledged. This will be very useful if the Egyptian Revolution, as is quite likely, actually starts to radicalise (in the socialist sense).

Even listing a few of the most obvious examples of loaded media language is a very long business: the way police deal "robustly" with "violent" protesters but police are never "violent"; how "our" soldiers are invariably "brave" and the enemy/terrorists are always "cowardly"; how politicians making cuts in education or social welfare are taking "hard decisions" and making "tough choices", but everyone, apart from extremists, knows that "in the real world" there "have to be cuts" and so on. Nor is it just a question of language: it is necessary to be aware that the camera can most certainly lie, that a camera angle can make a half empty meeting look packed or a small crowd look like a mass demonstration, and that the juxtaposition of news items in a bulletin affects their perception, while the connection not made (for example between "natural" disasters such as fires, floods and droughts, and climate change) can be just as important as the connections made.

But combating the media in one's head involves far more than just spotting its tricks and decoding its language; it involves having access to alternative sources of information and opinion, and ultimately it means developing an alternative worldview.

There have always been alternative sources: books, libraries, radical magazines and newspapers—everything from scholarly tomes by Marx and Chomsky and journals like *New Left Review* or *International Socialism* to popular pamphlets and papers sold on the streets like *Socialist Worker*. Of course this takes a certain amount of work— more work than simply accepting what the BBC or the *Sun* serves up on a plate, and more work than many people, preoccupied with the problems of daily life, are prepared to put in; nevertheless the information required for a critical reading of the media is, by and large, out there. The internet undoubtedly makes things easier, especially as regards gaining information internationally. With a few clicks of the mouse I can find out something about what is going on in Greece, Egypt or Australia regardless of whether the BBC or my newspaper has chosen to cover that part of the world today. I can also access basic factual information—dates, statistics, etc—very easily and pick up on a range of views via blogs of various kinds. And, if I'm prepared to dig, a wealth of research is available online.

However, the internet also exacerbates what was already a problem: not so much a lack of information as too much. By the time a book appears in a library it has, at least, passed through several quality control filters. This is not the case with much internet material. So how, out of the vast array of information and opinion on offer, does an individual distinguish what is relevant from what is irrelevant and determine what is true, what is untrue and what is half true? There are two main answers to this question: the first is that it is very difficult to do alone and is made much more effective if the task is undertaken as a collective endeavour by a group, community or organisation who share information and ideas (I shall return to this point); the second is that it requires the development of an alternative worldview or theory which provides a more or less coherent understanding of the world and a framework within which specific facts and stories can be located. At the very least this makes it possible to screen out large amounts of nonsense.

An example of the need for such theory is provided by the current prevalence of what are generally called "conspiracy theories". The main characteristics of conspiracy theories are: (a) they claim that the world is run by a very small number of people who are united and control more or less everything that happens; (b) that knowledge of this conspiracy is both deeply secret and quite widely available, including, naturally, to the conspiracy theorist concerned. These propositions are false and seriously misleading.

Of course it is true that Britain, the United States and every other country is run by a minority of its population and that minority are rich and powerful. But it is not true that they are a mere handful of secret individuals. No modern society, not even regimes headed by an individual dictator like Hitler, Stalin or Mubarak, can be run by a handful of people—a whole layer or social class consisting of tens or hundreds of thousands is required, because they have to be capable of controlling not only the large and complex state apparatus but also the main productive processes in the economy, the factories, mines, stores, companies and so on. Secondly, this class of rulers is not organised in a secretly manipulated hierarchy, but is bound together by common vested interests, essentially their share of the profits made out of the labour of working people. This means that despite their common class interest, as against the rest of us, these rulers find their unity disrupted by numerous conflicts, contradictions, and fault lines: the US versus China, BP versus Shell, Tesco versus Sainsbury, the *Daily Mail* versus the *Daily Express*, all the way down to rivalries between individuals; and they continually face resistance from below, from oppressed nations and exploited peoples. As a consequence, although they dominate the world and are mostly able to protect their interests, these rulers by no means control everything that happens in it. What actually happens—history—is the result not of a single will or force but of a multitude of conflicting forces. What is needed to understand the world and counter the media is not hidden knowledge of some secret conspiracy but a realistic analysis of these forces and what drives them.

This is what makes Marxism by far the most important, coherent and powerful of the alternatives to the capitalist or bourgeois ideology that dominates the mainstream media, and the most effective framework for reading the media against the grain. Marxism is not a conspiracy theory but a theory of class struggle. It argues that at the foundation of any society lies the way it organises production—the mode of production or economic base. Today that is capitalism, which divides people into those who do the work and live by selling their labour power (the working class, which includes most so-called white collar workers such as teachers and local government workers) and those who live by the profits they extract from the labour of the workers (the capitalists or employers who together form the ruling class) with various middle class layers in between. The interests of these classes are in conflict. The ruling class consists of real people, who often know each other and who from time to time do conspire, but what drives them and constrains them is the competitive pursuit of profit.

The mainstream media presents the world from the point of view of these rulers (even when it does so with a working class accent). Marxism analyses the world from the opposite point of the view, the standpoint of the working class, which forms an excellent basis for its critique.

## Using the capitalist media

I have devoted quite an amount of time to how we combat the media for ourselves, but of course what is needed is to be able to challenge the general social influence of the media. I have already argued against collaborating with the media on its own terms but that doesn't mean we shouldn't make use of it when the opportunity arises. Provided we don't forget that the mainstream media are enemy territory and don't allow appeasement of the media to dominate our activity, then it is essential for people who want change to intervene in the media in various ways.

These range from the very simple writing of letters to the papers (more useful generally than writing to MPs or ministers) or taking part in phone-ins, to issuing press releases on behalf of campaigns, being interviewed about demonstrations, and appearing either in the audience or on the panel of discussion programmes. All these activities are useful and are, of course, widely practised but it should be noted that for radicals these opportunities are likely to be quite restricted. It should also be noted that, apart from just writing letters, most of them involve and depend on some form of collective political organisation.

When discussing using the capitalist media it is necessary to remember that media producers, like virtually every workplace, company or institution in this society, are organised on the basis of a class hierarchy stretching from the owners and senior executives at the top to the caretakers and cleaning staff at the bottom. What is important here is that the majority of people who work in the press, TV, radio, etc are working class people who live by the sale of their labour power and are exploited by their employers in same way that call centre workers or factory workers are. This includes the majority of journalists, not all, of course—some are raised far above that level and are or become thoroughly bourgeois—but the majority. The National Union of Journalists is a bona fide part of the workers' movement and has sometimes had quite left wing general secretaries.

This means that it is quite possible for some people to become left wing journalists in press or broadcasting and thereby to exercise a small influence on the overall output. Mostly this happens fairly low down the food chain, and is subject to all sorts of control by sub-editors, editors, producers, etc. Nevertheless there are a few instances of journalists who, partly because of their outstanding abilities, rise quite high in the profession and become well known, while retaining their principles and critical practice: Paul Foot, John Pilger, Eamonn McCann and Robert Fisk are obvious examples. And there are parallel figures in other branches of the media such as Ken Loach and Michael Moore in film-making or Mark Thomas and Mark Steel in TV comedy. But, inevitably, such individuals remain a tiny minority unable to alter the overall capitalist character of the media and for each of these principled individuals there are others, like Christopher Hitchens or Julie Burchill, who change their tune when they get, or in order to get, a whiff of fame and fortune.

It also means that there is a possibility of collective action by media workers on issues beyond their own pay and conditions. In 1972 the Heath Conservative government jailed five dockers, known as the Pentonville Five, for picketing. The dockers then turned to the print workers for support and the whole of Fleet Street (all the national newspapers) shut down in solidarity—this had a massive political and ideological impact and set the scene for a general strike which was called by the TUC but averted by the capitulation of the government. In the Great Miners' Strike of 1984-5, the *Sun* tried to run a front page purporting to show the miners' leader, Arthur Scargill, giving a Nazi salute (in fact he was just waving to someone) combined with the headline "Mine Fuhrer". The compositors (print workers) simply refused to set the page and the *Sun* ran without it. During the Iraq war an organisation called Media Workers Against the War was set up, with the support of some of the above named journalists, and it made a significant contribution to the general anti-war movement. However, such struggles by media workers are relatively rare and tend to occur in the context of much wider class struggles and movements—a point to which I shall return.

## Internet and social media

Given the huge hype Facebook and Twitter have received recently—they have widely been given credit for the Egyptian Revolution and even the whole Arab Spring, as well as the Spanish *indignados* movement—they are hardly in need of a recommendation in this booklet; it is more important to stress their limitations. Nevertheless I know there are people on the left who still shy away from using these technologies so I will start by making a simple point: they are means of communication and it makes no more sense to fail to use them than it would to have refused to use the telephone when it first became available.

Moreover the internet in general and Facebook and Twitter

in particular, have certain important advantages for radicals. Compared to what is normally meant by the mass media, ie TV, newspapers, radio, films, etc, they are decentred in their operation and therefore much harder to control. Instead of simply being a means whereby a very small number of (highly privileged) people can talk to the rest of us, they are a means whereby large numbers of people can talk to each other. Also, although they are by no means free, the cost of using them is minimal compared to the cost of establishing a newspaper or TV or radio station, or even talking on the phone. In this sense they are potentially a democratising force. They are especially useful in the way they facilitate rapid international communication by ordinary people. As Jonny Jones has commented in his excellent article on "Social Media and Social Movements" in *International Socialism* 130:

> The speed at which information has travelled from continent to continent, partly propelled by activists utilising the internet, has allowed for such images as that of the protester in Tahrir Square, surrounded by Egyptian flags, holding up a placard reading "Egypt Supports Wisconsin Workers" to be spread across the world.[43]

Another good example of the power of new technologies, in this case of YouTube, comes from the *indignados* movement in Barcelona. On 15 June 2011 an anti-cuts protest was held at the Catalan parliament. Up to then the movement had been peaceful but on this occasion it appeared to turn violent and was, of course, roundly denounced for this by the mainstream media. However, the protesters had captured video footage proving that the violence was instigated by police agent provocateurs in the crowd.[44] Within hours this was out on YouTube and went viral. On Sunday 19 June up to a million people across Spain marched in support of the protesters.

So obviously the best use possible should be made of all these new tools of communication, just as it should of all the old tools like the spoken word and the book. But what about the limitations?

First it is a mistake to attribute the Egyptian Revolution of 2011, or the British student revolt of 2010, the Spanish revolt or any other mass movement to these new technologies as if they were the cause or the main factors in the events. The French Revolution of 1789 used the newspapers (notably Marat's *L'Ami du Peuple*) but it wasn't a "paper revolution". The Russian Revolution of 1917 also used newspapers and then, after the event, film (for example Eisenstein's *Battleship Potemkin*) but it wasn't either a paper or a film revolution. May 1968 in Paris used silk screen posters yet it wasn't a "silk screen revolution". The main factor in any such upheaval or great historical process is the people who make it and their social position and situation—rising bourgeois plus *sans culottes* in the French Revolution, workers and peasants in the Russian Revolution, students and workers in May '68, the youth and workers in Egypt, and so on.

Second, although Facebook, Twitter and YouTube are often called "social media" they are in fact capitalist media just like Disney or Time Warner or News Corp. I said above they are relatively decentred in operation but they are not decentred in ultimate ownership and control. Google Inc is an American multinational corporation with 24,400 employees, profit in 2010 of $8.5 billion and total assets of $57.8 billion. Facebook is privately owned by Facebook Inc, which in turn is partly owned by Goldman Sachs. It has 2,000 employees and an estimated revenue in 2010 of $2 billion. Twitter was launched in 2006, has 450 employees and projected revenue of $140 million in 2010. YouTube LLC was set up in 2005 in California and was bought by Google Inc for $1.65 billion in 2006.

This matters because all of these companies make their

money through advertising and all can, if they choose, censor their output. Likewise they can all be blocked by states. There are economic incentives not to do this for both the companies and governments but if push comes to shove both sides will do it. Thus in July 2010 Google did a deal with the Chinese government to get its internet license renewed by accepting Beijing's insistence that it must not provide outlawed information, presumably because it did not want to lose out on the lucrative Chinese market. YouTube has been blocked at various times by China, Morocco, Thailand, Turkey and others. Most spectacularly Egypt on 25 January unplugged itself entirely from the internet in a bid to stop the revolutionaries communicating with each other, with the population and the world.

All of this shows that it would be a mistake to place the use of social media at the centre of any strategy for social change but the last example also shows why there is no need to. For when the Egyptian government shut down the internet, the mobilisations of the Egyptian people simply increased and intensified with communication taking place by poster, leaflet, graffiti, and most importantly by word of mouth. Sameh Naguib in his superb pamphlet, *The Egyptian Revolution: A Political Analysis and Eyewitness Account* (Bookmarks, 2011), testifies that once the numbers demonstrating crossed a certain threshold just hearing the slogan "The people want to bring down the regime!" echoing in the poorer districts of Cairo brought people who certainly didn't have PCs or Facebook accounts pouring into the streets.

A third simple fact is that if this technology can be used to combat or get round the influence of the mainstream media from the left it also can be, and is, used for the same purpose from the right. For every radical blog or website there can be a right wing blog or website. If protesting students are on Facebook so are the BNP and the English Defence League. For every Hossam el-Hamalawy and Gigi Ibrahim (Egyptian revolutionaries and bloggers) there will be a Salafist blogger I haven't heard of (the Salafis are right wing Islamist counter revolutionaries). If the net can link Wisconsin and Tahrir Square it can also link the Ku Klux Klan with German Neo-Nazis and Anders Breivik with the EDL.

The fact that radical interpretations of the potential of the new media are currently in the ascendant is because over the last year movements for change have, by and large, been in the ascendant rather than movements of reaction and the right. Ultimately it is what is happening in the real world, in the streets, the squares and the workplaces, not the virtual world, that is decisive.

Finally there are some specific problems associated with online communication which are highly problematic for the left. On the one hand there is a tendency on Facebook and in the blogosphere to engage in sectarian bickering and crude insult (safe in the knowledge you can't get punched on the nose) which does no one any good. On the other hand there can develop a culture of signing up for causes and groups in cyberspace and promising to attend events with no real intention of turning up, in a way that becomes a substitute for any real activity.

I would therefore endorse Jonny Jones's balanced judgement that "the internet and social media are often a useful complement to the kinds of activism that the left has traditionally engaged in. Where online activism has been seen as a replacement for this kind of activity, it has been unsuccessful".[45]

## Mass struggle

The struggle against the power and influence of the capitalist media cannot be waged in isolation from a wider struggle to change society. Central to both is mass action and ultimately mass revolutionary action. Everything I have argued so far points to this conclusion. Media bias is the way it is because it is part of, and reflects, the overall structure of power in society. The influence of the media over people's thinking is at its weakest when there is mass resistance and the masses themselves are actors in the events, "the news" that is being reported. Conditions of mass struggle are also the conditions in which people's minds will most open up to the alternative world view—socialism and Marxism—which best enables them to read the capitalist media against the grain.

Mass struggle gives working people a sense of their own potential power—power which the media, along with the rest of society, normally denies—and this raises their confidence. With higher levels of confidence come wider horizons, the ability to tackle and grasp new ideas. Prejudice and bigotry are undermined—in mass struggle it becomes much clearer who the real enemy are and the need for scapegoats fades.

The Egyptian Revolution has provided fresh examples of this process: how Muslims and Christians united in Tahrir Square defending each other's prayers; how men and women (some veiled, others unveiled) fought, lived and slept alongside each other in the occupation.

The Egyptian Revolution also provides fascinating examples of how when the masses are mobilised all sorts of practical problems are solved. When you have hundreds of thousands occupying a vast square one real problem is where to pee, but when you have hundreds of thousands involved they include plumbers and builders who can improvise public toilets. Another problem is how to charge mobile phones, but the masses include electricians and telephone engineers who can dig up the pavement and tap into the underground cables.

The involvement of the masses in revolutionary action makes it possible to raise the struggle against the capitalist media to whole new levels. The best examples of this come from the Portuguese Revolution of 1974-5. It is a testimony to the media's power of exclusion of any anti-capitalist narrative that almost no one under 40 even knows there was such a thing as the Portuguese Revolution. It began with a left wing military coup against the 40-year fascist dictatorship of Salazar and Caetano, unleashed a mass movement of workers and soldiers from below, and saw the highest levels of working class revolutionary struggle anywhere in Western Europe since the Spanish Civil War of 1936-7.

> In this small country the attendance on some demonstrations exceeded half a million. In the working class bars political discussion and argument were intense... Workers discussed the situation in France, in England, Argentina, Brazil as if they'd been professors of politics all their lives. Posters advocating armed insurrection were legal. Even the bus tickets had political slogans on them.
>
> The commanders of the state could no longer rely on its army. Tanks rumbled in cobbled streets alongside, and carrying, demonstrating workers. The scale of the factory occupations recalled France in 1936 and 1968... And not only the factories were taken over. Popular clinics and cultural centres mushroomed. In one hospital the workers took over from the nuns, and invited them to come and vote at the mass meetings.[46]

In this situation, as Tony Cliff observed at the time, "One of the foremost working-class battles—important economically, politically and ideologically—was over control of the media".[47] This included the workers' strike and occupation at the Fascist-run *Jornal do Comercio*, which began in April 1974 and lasted until the end of August. During the occupation the workers published a strike paper and were supported by a one-day general strike at other Lisbon dailies. This was followed by the occupation of *Republica*, a paper edited by Paul Rego, minister of information and leader of the (pro-capitalist) Socialist Party. Most important was the workers' takeover of the Catholic church's Radio Renascenca (the leading radio station in Portugal) which took place in early 1975. The station was put at the disposal of the working class. Writing at the time, Tony Cliff describes its output:

> The programming of the station is done by a general assembly. Reports of struggles all over the world are regularly broadcast. The struggles going on in the factories, tenants' committees and so on are given a wide hearing.[48]

Of course, with the collapse of the revolution at the end of 1975 and the return of Portuguese society to capitalist "normality" these media outlets were also returned to business as usual.

It is clear that the battle for control of the media is likely to be a key issue in any modern revolution, and that all sorts of initiatives are possible.

## Political organisation

Mass struggle is the single most important factor in combating the influence and challenging the power of the media but in the end it is not enough on its own. It needs to be complemented and accompanied by political organisation. By political organisation I mean everything from trade unionism, to local and national campaigns, to the organisation of a fully-fledged revolutionary socialist party.

The class that controls the media at present, and in whose interests it operates, is extremely well organised politically. In the first place it possesses the various apparatuses of the state—armed forces, police, judiciary—all of which have excellent access to the media and close working relationships with it. Then it has numerous business associations like the CBI and the Institute of Directors, think tanks, and professional associations—all capable of influencing the media. And of course it has its political parties. In every country the capitalist class has at least one major party which it finances and which more or less unambiguously pursues its interests. In Britain it is, of course, the Conservative Party; in Germany the Christian Democrats; in France the Union for a Popular Movement. In some countries, notably the US with the Republicans and the Democrats, it has two major parties. Therefore, working people and anti-capitalist forces also need their own forms of political organisation and these play a crucial role in the struggle against the media at every level.

At the level of combating the media in one's own head it is clear that this is more effectively done together with other people, rather than on one's own. Any organisation, any trade union or campaign will be a source of alternative information and able to generate and share its own research. Most effective in this regard is a socialist political party because it will be able to present alternative information and an alternative view across the board, not just on a single issue or narrow range of issues. This in turn will impact on, inform and strengthen the use of the capitalist media from letter writing to appearances on TV programmes, the use of the internet, Facebook and Twitter and the ideological struggle as a whole. The Italian Marxist Antonio Gramsci, who stressed that ruling class power was always a combination of "force and consent, authority and hegemony",[49] and had to be contested at both levels, also insisted that a political party was a necessity for waging this struggle. "The modern prince [a reference to Machiavelli's *The Prince* in which he called for a leader to emerge as a builder of the Italian nation]...can only be an organism, a complex element of society in which a collective will, which has already been recognised and has to some extent asserted itself in action, begins to take concrete form.

History has already provided this mechanism and it is the political party".[50]

One of the functions of such a party is to produce its own media, publications that are completely independent of the capitalist state or class and not dependent on advertising or sponsorship but able to put forward a clear and uncompromising critique of the system. Historically, from the French Revolution onwards, this has meant, first and foremost, producing a newspaper. Jean Paul Marat's *L'Ami du Peuple* was the prototype, followed by the Chartists' *Northern Star* and *Red Republican* in the first half of the 19th century. Marx, in the European revolutions of 1848, had the *Neue Rheinische Zeitung* (New Rhineland Gazette) and Lenin and the Bolsheviks had first *Iskra* (the Spark) and then *Pravda* (Truth). Gramsci had *L'Ordine Nuovo* (New Order) and the Communist Party of Great Britain in its earlier years had the *Daily Worker* (later the *Morning Star*). The SWP has *Socialist Worker*.*

What all these papers had in common was that they tried to combine fighting for an alternative worldview with organising their supporters and those they influenced to take action. Both these tasks have to be performed at various levels. Comments on the main events of the day and popular exposures of ruling class abuses have to be complemented by broader historical and theoretical articles. Drawing workers into producing and identifying with the paper, through letters and strike reports, needs to go hand in hand with publicising meetings and demonstrations, running campaigns, mobilising solidarity for disputes and trying to give a concrete lead to the movement by answering the question,

---

\* Chris Harman provides a useful historical overview of these and other radical papers in "The Revolutionary Press", *International Socialism* 24 (summer 1984), http://www.marxists.org/archive/harman/1984/xx/revpress.html#top

WILL THE REVOLUTION BE TELEVISED?

"What needs to be done next?"

Recently a number of commentators have suggested that, because of electronic media, the day of the newspaper is over. But there are two substantial objections to this. The first is that many working class people continue to read newspapers and don't have access to online material and the second is that selling a newspaper allows for personal contact and dialogue with workers, students and activists in a way that cyber-space does not. However it is also clear that no contemporary radical party is going to communicate solely through its newspaper but will also need to use the full potential of modern technology.

The main point on which I want to conclude is that the five strategic elements outlined here need to be combined in such a way as to reinforce each other.

# 6. The media after capitalism

It is not possible to predict or prescribe in any concrete detail how the media will be organised or what form it will take in post-capitalist society. This will depend on the circumstances obtaining and technology available when such a society comes into being, and on the will and choices of the people of the future. Neither of these can possibly be known at present. So why write about it at all?

In the first place because having sharply criticised the existing capitalist media and rejected the possibility of substantially changing or reforming it under capitalism it seems incumbent on me to offer, at least, a broad outline of what I would like to see as an alternative and would advocate working towards. In the second place I am very aware of an obvious and standard right wing objection to the arguments presented here: namely that, whatever Molyneux or any other radical critics of the media may say, the only real alternative to a media dominated by the free market and capitalist competition would be one dominated by the state which would turn out to be monolithic and totalitarian party or government propaganda as in Communist Russia.

This objection derives from one of the central arguments advanced in defence of capitalism and against socialism—namely that capitalism and freedom are completely interdependent and that the only possible alternative to "free enterprise" and private ownership of businesses is state ownership, which goes hand in hand with bureaucratic oppression and dictatorship. This in turn rests on the assumption, sometimes overt sometimes covert, that it is impossible for the mass of ordinary people to really exercise collective democratic control over society in anything but the most limited sense of electing a parliamentary government every four or five years; that it is impossible for working people to democratically control industry or schools or hospitals, or to produce a democratic plan for the economy, either because of their intellectual incapacity (which is seldom said openly these days) or because of human nature which is programmed for greed and hierarchy (which is said a great deal).

Now obviously Marx and anti-Stalinist socialists believe otherwise. The debate is a fundamental one and I can't rehearse it all here (I have written on it elsewhere—John Molyneux, *Is Human Nature a Barrier to Socialism?* London, 1993) but the basic points are simple. First, archaeological and anthropological evidence shows that for more than 95 percent of their history human beings lived as hunter-gatherers in non profit driven, non-market, non-hierarchical, egalitarian societies based on the sharing of gathered and hunted food. So it is demonstrably false that humans are programmed or genetically hard wired for greed, inequality and absence of democracy. Second, experience—under capitalism—shows that ordinary people are capable of both greedy and unselfish behaviour, of narrow self-interest and generous solidarity, of servile deference and defiant insistence on their democratic rights. Both modes of behaviour are part of human nature; which predominates depends very much on circumstances and social conditions. The social conditions of hunting and gathering favoured sharing and equality; those of capitalism favour greed and (massive) inequality—indeed for the ruling capitalist class they make it obligatory. The structure of socialist society would actively encourage collectivity and democracy and consciously prevent privilege and undemocratic hierarchy.

But doesn't the example of the Russian Revolution prove that democratic socialism and equality are impossible dreams? Actually the Russian Revolution itself, in which ordinary people—workers, soldiers, sailors, peasants—rose to extraordinary heights of solidarity and self-sacrifice and created mass workers' councils ("soviet" is just the Russian for council), which were exemplary instruments of democratic workers' power, shows exactly the opposite. The degeneration of the revolution into Stalinist dictatorship, however, shows the impossibility of creating and sustaining a socialist society in one country alone, surrounded by a hostile capitalist world—a fact foreseen and predicted by Marx, Engels, Lenin and Trotsky, indeed by all the classical Marxists before Stalin.* As for Eastern Europe, China, North Korea, Cuba, etc, in these countries the workers' revolution from below that occurred in Russia in 1917 was absent. Instead there was, in all these countries, a military takeover at the top without mass mobilisations from below and the imposition of one-party Stalinist rule (essentially state capitalism) from the outset.†

So what about the media in post-capitalist society, by which I mean in the immediate aftermath of an anti-capitalist revolution? Let us grant for the moment (I will qualify this later) that today's major media corporations and outlets—the Murdoch empire, the Rothermere stable, BSkyB, ITV, etc, etc—will be taken into public, ie state, ownership. Will this produce an open and democratic media? It all depends on the character of

---

\* There is a vast Marxist literature on the Russian Revolution and its degeneration, in particular, Leon Trotsky, *The History of the Russian Revolution* (London, 1977), and *The Revolution Betrayed* (London, 1967), Tony Cliff, *State Capitalism in Russia* (London, 1974), Chris Harman, "Russia: How the Revolution was Lost", *International Socialism* 30 (autumn 1967), http://www.marxists.de/statecap/harman/revlost.htm, John Molyneux, "What is the Real Marxist Tradition?", *International Socialism* 20 (summer 1983), http://www.marxisme.dk/arkiv/molyneux/realmarx/index.htm

† See Chris Harman, *Class Struggles in Eastern Europe 1945-83* (London, 1983), and John Molyneux, "What is the Real Marxist Tradition?" as above.

the state that will own and control it.

Writing in 1871, on the basis of the experience of the Paris Commune when the working people of Paris took over the running of the city for 74 days, Marx formulated some basic principles for a democratic workers' state. First he noted that "the working class cannot simply lay hold of the ready-made state machinery, and wield it for its own purposes";[51] rather it has to get rid of the old state apparatus and replace it with its own. "The first decree of the Commune, therefore, was the suppression of the standing army, and the substitution for it of the armed people".[52]

The Commune was formed of the municipal councillors, chosen by universal suffrage in the various wards of the town, responsible and revocable at short terms. The majority of its members were naturally working men, or acknowledged representatives of the working class. The Commune was to be a working body, executive and legislative at the same time.

Instead of continuing to be the agent of the central government, the police force was at once stripped of its political attributes, and turned into the responsible, and at all times revocable, agent of the Commune. So were the officials of all other branches of the administration. From the members of the Commune downwards, public service had to be done at workman's wages. The vested interests and the representation allowances of the high dignitaries of state disappeared along with the high dignitaries themselves.

Two extremely important ideas here are the revocability of all officials and representatives, and that public service had to be done at workers' wages. These were measures specifically designed to block careerism and any emergence of a new elite. I would argue that these principles remain valid today as the basis for a highly democratic and egalitarian post-capitalist administration. An additional factor comes from the workers' councils of the Russian Revolution—that members of the soviets were elected not primarily from geographical wards but from workplaces and soldiers' barracks, ie from collectives where debate could take place and where meetings of electors could much more easily be convened than in a parliamentary constituency. This innovation greatly strengthens the principle of recallability and democratic control from below.

A mass media run by such a state would be infinitely more democratic than one run by Rupert Murdoch, the BBC or Richard Desmond. There is no reason at all why it should be monolithic or dominated by one party. The notion of a one-party state was first forced on the Bolsheviks as a temporary measure in the extremely desperate circumstances of civil war and then adopted as a principle by Stalinism as an instrument of repression by the new ruling class. It had no place in Marx's (or Lenin's) conception of socialism and it should have no place in ours. Rather workers' councils allow for the representation within them of many parties according to the degree of their support among the people and this range of views would be reflected in the media.

Earlier in this booklet I argued that the BBC is an instrument not of a neutral state but of a capitalist state and therefore is deeply pro-capitalist in its stance. But it is certainly no less, and arguably a good deal more, democratic and pluralist in its conduct and content than the privately owned Fox News or Murdoch press or *Daily Express*. Therefore there is no reason why public service media in a democratically organised post-capitalist society should not be even more so.

Of course there would have to be some restrictions. At present in Britain open incitement of race hatred is not allowed in the media or society (which doesn't mean there isn't a lot of coded or covert incitement). I do not believe racism, for example, would be allowed in the media of the new society. If anything the limits would be stricter than they are now because the new society would have a great need for solidarity and could not afford to split on racial or national or religious lines. But this would not mean that all sorts of political debates would not take place. In the immediate aftermath of anti-capitalist revolution it would probably be necessary to ban incitement to counter-revolution, especially if the new society was being actively threatened with armed intervention or violent attempts to restore the old order. But I think there would be no need for this to be more than temporary because once the new society is firmly established, especially when it has become international, people advocating a return to the past would be as ineffectual and harmless as people who now who want to go back to feudalism and the romance of the Middle Ages. Even allowing for these restrictions the media would, in reality, be far freer than a media completely dominated by billionaires.

Also, although the central media outlets would be publicly owned, they would be accompanied and "surrounded" by numerous independent smaller ventures organised by community groups, trade unions, pensioners associations, student associations, political groups, collectives and individuals of all kinds, which could be grant aided or self-funded. To some extent this happens already but the "independents" are at a huge disadvantage compared to the major corporations with their greatly superior technology (because of vastly greater capital investment), their mass advertising and so on. A more equal society would make for a much more level playing field. Moreover, the new technologies of communication based on the internet, which are likely to advance at a considerable rate, are more interactive than the dominant technologies of the 20th century (the press, film, radio and TV) and thus potentially conducive to democracy. A society characterised by democratic control from below which wanted actively to encourage political participation and active involvement in decision making would find a useful tool in social media.

At present most working people actively dislike "politics" because experience teaches them that what they say and think is ignored—that it makes no difference. As we have noted, this alienation makes many people look to the media more for entertainment than for information, news or debate. If ordinary people were actively involved in making real decisions that affected their lives—shall we focus on building schools or hospitals instead of hotels, is the priority at the moment nursery, primary or secondary education, do we need more trams or buses or a new underground line and so on—this would transform their attitude to politics and therefore to the media.

In the longer run the successful construction of a socialist society would bring with it a massive raising of the educational and cultural level of the people and an overcoming of the alienation which feeds some of the ugliest features of the media at present. It would mean, I believe, that the demand for the sleazy sensationalism of the *Sun* and the *Daily Star*, the celebrity worship of *OK!* and *Hello!*, the voyeurism of *Big Brother* and the vicarious wish fulfilment of *The X Factor* would shrink and wither away.

Just as the struggle against the existing capitalist media cannot be separated from the wider struggle to change society, so the making of a new media would be part of the making of a new society. But given success in this enterprise there is no reason why we should not be able to create a mass, democratic, truthful and interactive media of high quality which would be as different from what we have at present as chalk from cheese.

# Appendix

*The Murdoch scandal—their media and ours*

There are a moments when a single event, like a flash of lightning, illuminates the sky and reveals the whole landscape below, which previously remained hidden in the dark. Such is the *News of the World* phone hacking scandal which has engulfed Rupert Murdoch and his whole News Corporation media empire. And what a landscape it has revealed!

Across the world we live in societies dominated and run by a small minority of their population. This ruling minority is not a tiny handful, some secret conspiratorial committee, but a definite social class consisting of the very rich, the industrialists, the bankers, the financiers, the generals, the judges, the police chiefs and so on—together they make up maybe 1, at most 2, percent of the population.

This class, which has a common interest in boosting profits, exploiting working people and defending capitalism, masks its domination through a division of labour. It spreads its members out through a variety of institutions which are claimed to be independent of each other.

The judges are independent. The police are independent. The politicians are independent. The state broadcasting corporation (BBC or RTE) is independent. The civil service is independent. The editors of newspapers are independent. The committees of inquiry, headed by independent judges, are independent. And they are all non-political except the politicians.

Moreover they all check and balance each other so that no one individual group or faction gets too much power, and everything is fair and democratic.

What the phone hacking scandal lit up was the murky world of the interconnections that, in practice, link all these institutions together. And what a murky world it is—key establishment figures left with hardly a fig leaf to cover their shame. "Tyrants, hypocrites, liars!" as Patrick Pearse described a previous generation of the British ruling class.

As the timeline below shows, the core of the scandal is simply that journalists working for Rupert Murdoch routinely illegally tapped people's phones. The scandal started to come out when they were caught hacking the phone of a member of the royal family. It exploded when it emerged they had hacked the phone of child murder victim Milly Dowler—that was too horrible to spin or sweep under the carpet.

As the scandal unravelled, however, it became clear that they were all in it together—Britain's top politicians, top police and top media producers. They were all politically and socially connected. Cameron had numerous private meetings with Murdoch and was a neighbour and friend, and they all protected each other, much the same as America protects its puppet dictators like Hosni Mubarak, until the last possible moment, quite regardless of any considerations of morality or decency.

We need to understand there is nothing unusual about this. It is how the system works. In Ireland Charley Haughey resigned over a phone tapping scandal, and was corruptly linked to Ben Dunne and AIB. Bertie Aherne was up to his neck in it with Haughey, like Brian Cowan with Seanie Fitzpatrick and Michael Lowry with Denis O'Brien, who with Tony O'Reilly controls most of this country's media.

Some commentators, like David McWilliams, have said this is "crony capitalism", not "real" capitalism. It's not; it is how capitalism operates in the real world from Texas to Beijing. Tony Blair and Gordon Brown were also linked to

Murdoch. George Bush and Dick Cheney were linked to the oil industry.

Capitalism oozes corruption like an athlete oozes sweat, for the simple reason that it is a system driven, first to last, by profit and ruled, not just by rotten individuals, but by a class which owns and controls the means of production and, on that basis, dominates economically, politically and ideologically.

At the same time, the scandal also shows that our rulers are not all powerful. They are beset by contradictions and rivalries among themselves and they fear the people. Faced with exposure and potential revolt they retreat and discard subordinates, Coulson here and Brooks there, to preserve those at the top. Faced with serious revolt or revolution, as in Egypt, they will even sacrifice those at the very top to save the system. But they can be beaten.

While every corrupt scalp taken is a step forward it is the system itself, capitalism, that has to be uprooted. And for this working people and socialists need our own media.

This is because the mainstream media is not only self-serving, dishonest and corrupt but also systematically promotes a pro-capitalist view of the world—a view which absolutely takes it for granted that production has to be organised for profit, that "the markets" have to be kept happy, and that "entrepreneurs", ie capitalists, are the real wealth creators.

We need a newspaper, like *Socialist Worker*, which reports on and reflects the struggles of working people—their strikes, demonstrations, campaigns and uprisings, here and in other countries—in a way RTE and the *Evening Herald* will never do.

But the paper has to do more than just record what is happening; it also to develop and communicate an alternative anti-capitalist, socialist world view. It has to expose the evils of capitalism but also explain how the system works. It has to fight against reactionary ideas that can divide the workers' movement, like racism, sexism and homophobia, and champion the oppressed such as travellers and refugees, who the capitalist media like to scapegoat.

It has to serve as the memory of the working class, preserving the history of our class's past struggles such as the Paris Commune, the Dublin Lockout, the Russian Revolution, and the workers' councils in Ireland during the War of Independence—a history which would otherwise be ignored and forgotten. It has to arm its readers with the political arguments to counter the propaganda of the politicians and make the case for a socialist alternative.

It also has to act as an organiser of the workers' movement, bringing groups of workers together, building solidarity and resistance to the system on every front. Finally it has to serve as a kind of scaffolding, within which a workers' socialist organisation, a party of the working class, is constructed and grows.

Of course other media—Facebook, Twitter, YouTube, film, etc—all can and should be used for these purposes too, but the paper remains key because of the way selling it enables socialists to interact with the workers' movement and other working people on a face to face basis.

## Timeline of the scandal

2000—*News of the World* (*NoW*) editor Rebekah Brooks launches campaigns against paedophiles and for public access to the Sex Offenders Register (known as Sarah's Law after murdered eight year old Sarah Payne).

2002—Schoolgirl Milly Dowler murdered.

2003—Brooks moves to the *Sun*. Andy Coulson becomes editor of *NoW*. Brooks admits to a parliamentary committee that she paid the police for information. News International says this is "not company practice".

2005—*NoW* runs story about Prince William's injured knee, based on intercepted phone messages. Royal officials complain and the police investigate.

2006-7—*NoW* royal editor Clive Goodman and private investigator Glen Mulcaire are arrested for hacking royal phones and, after guilty pleas, are jailed for four and six months respectively. Andy Coulson resigns as editor but says he knew nothing.

May 2007—Coulson becomes Conservative Party director of communications under David Cameron.

2008—News International pays Gordon Taylor of the Professional Footballers Association £700,000 to settle phone hacking claim.

2009—Brooks becomes CEO of News International. It emerges that *NoW* reporters, with knowledge of senior staff, hacked the phones of celebrities and politicians while Coulson was editor from 2003 to 2007 and that the company had paid out more than £1 million to settle phone hacking cases. Scotland Yard announced it would not be carrying out a new investigation into the allegations.

*NoW* editor Colin Myler, Coulson (again) and Les Hinton (chair of Dow Jones and Murdoch's right hand man) all deny evidence of phone hacking beyond the one case that had come to court. The Press Complaints Commission accepts this.

2010—In January House of Commons Media Committee says it was inconceivable that the *NoW* management didn't know about phone hacking, but in May Coulson becomes director of communications for new Con-Dem government.

Accusations of hacking pile up, from actress Sienna Miller (who wins a settlement of £100,000), MP George Galloway, union leader Bob Crow, former deputy PM John Prescott, MP Chris Bryant, footballer Ryan Giggs and journalist Brendan Montague.

December 2010—Crown Prosecution Service says there will be no more prosecutions and Cameron continues to defend Coulson despite calls for his resignation by Prescott and others.

2011—In January Coulson resigns. In March three senior *NoW* journalists are arrested but bailed till September. News International starts to apologise. Pressure continues to mount. Ryan Giggs launches legal action, Andy Gray receives a settlement of £20,000. Prescott calls for a public inquiry.

4 July—The flash of lightning! Evidence emerges that they hacked the phone of Milly Dowler while she was missing and misled her parents into thinking she was still alive.

5-6 July—Claims surface in relation to Soham parents, victims of the 7/7 terrorist attacks and relatives of soldiers killed in Iraq and Afghanistan. But Murdoch still backs Rebekah Brooks.

7 July—News Corp announces the closure of the *News of the World*.

8 July—Coulson is arrested and former royal editor Clive Goodman is rearrested (over payments to police).

12 July—Scotland Yard deputy commissioner John Yates (responsible for 2009 decision not to reopen inquiry) tells parliament he won't resign.

13 July—Murdoch withdraws his bid for BSkyB.

14 July—Neil Wallis, former *NoW* executive editor, is arrested. In the *Wall Street Journal*, which he owns, Murdoch says, "Some minor mistakes have been made."

15 July—Rebekah Brooks resigns.

17 July—Sir Paul Stephenson, Metropolitan police commissioner, resigns, followed next day by his deputy, John Yates. It is now suggested that the mother of paedophile victim Sarah Payne—back where this story started—had her phone hacked by her "friend" Rebekah Brooks.

**First published in *Socialist Worker* (Ireland), August 2011.**

# Notes

1.  http://www.guardian.co.uk/media/gallery/2011/aug/09/uk-riots-front-pages-in-pictures#/?picture=377707624&index=0

2.  http://www.youtube.com/watch?v=biJgILxGK0o

3.  http://www.thesun.co.uk/sol/homepage/news/sun_says/244723/The-Sun-Says.html

4.  http://www.dailymail.co.uk/news/article-2023898/London-riots-Red-sky-night-Tottenhams-alight.html

5.  http://www.dailymail.co.uk/debate/article-2028417/DOUGLAS-CARSWELL-These-people-shoplifters-looters--looted-society.html#ixzz1VfCXhglf

6.  http://www.mirror.co.uk/news/top-stories/2011/08/13/uk-riots-tony-parsons-the-britain-we-knew-has-gone-for-ever-115875-23340566/

7.  http://www.defensenews.com/story.php?i=466197

8.  http://orwell.ru/library/novels/1984/english/en_p_2

9.  See http://pubs.socialistreviewindex.org.uk/isj98/sparks.htm

10. http://www.bbc.co.uk/news/business-13346599

11. http://en.wikipedia.org/wiki/List_of_UK_game_shows

12. Cited in C Geraghty, *Women and Soap Opera: A Study of Prime-Time Soaps* (London, 1991), p32.

13. F Engels, Letter to Margaret Harkness, April 1888, http://www.marxists.org/archive/marx/works/1888/letters/88_04_15.htm There are, of course, much more developed Marxist conceptions of "realism" in relation to literature and culture. See for example Georg Lukács, *The Meaning of Contemporary Realism* (London, 1979), and Mike Wayne, "Theses on Realism and Film", *International Socialism* 116 (autumn 2007).

14. http://en.wikipedia.org/wiki/Mark_Fowler

15. http://stats.bis.gov.uk/UKSA/tu/TUM2010.pdf

16. http://www.towerhamlets.gov.uk/lgsl/901-950/916_borough_

statistics.aspx

17. http://www.statistics.gov.uk/cci/nugget.asp?id=455

18. James Curran, "Advertising and the Press", cited in E Herman and N Chomsky, *Manufacturing Consent* (London, 1988), p15.

19. As above, p17.

20. John Berger, *Ways of Seeing* (London, 1988), pp129-154.

21. Naomi Klein, *No Logo* (London, 2000), p11.

22. "It's official: class matters", *Guardian*, 28 February 2006.

23. "Social class determines child's success", *Independent*, 18 September 2008.

24. http://www.marxists.org/archive/marx/works/1844/manuscripts/labour.htm

25. Karl Marx, *Capital*, Vol 1 (London, 1974), p41.

26. http://www.vanityfair.com/culture/features/2008/10/wolff200810?intcmp=239#gotopage2

27. Karl Marx and Frederick Engels, *The German Ideology* (London, 1985), p48.

28. Karl Marx, "Preface to A Contribution to the Critique of Political Economy", in D McLellan, *Karl Marx: Selected Writings* (Oxford, 1977), p389.

29. Frederick Engels, Letter to Borgius, 1894, http://www.marxists.org/archive/marx/works/1894/letters/94_01_25.htm

30. http://en.wikipedia.org/wiki/List_of_companies_by_revenue

31. http://money.cnn.com/magazines/fortune/global500/2011/full_list/

32. http://media.ft.com/cms/33558890-98d4-11e0-bd66-00144feab49a.pdf

33. Figures taken from the Broadcasters' Audience Research Board, http://www.barb.co.uk/report/weeklyViewing?_s=4

34. http://en.wikipedia.org/wiki/List_of_newspapers_in_the_United_Kingdom_by_circulation#Circulation_in_the_2000s

35. http://www.marxists.org/archive/marx/works/1845/german-ideology/ch01b.htm

36. Sameh Naguib, *The Egyptian Revolution: A Political Analysis and Eyewitness Account* (London, 2011).

37. http://thewestislamandsharia.blogspot.com/2011/04/poll-egyptians-positive-about-future.html

38. http://www.guardian.co.uk/media/greenslade/2011/feb/10/dailystar-english-defence-league

39. W L Miller, *Media and the Voters: The Audience, Content and Influence of the Press and TV at the 1987 General Election* (Oxford, 1991), pp164-165.

40. D Morley, *Television, Audiences and Cultural Studies* (London, 1988), p117.

41. Leon Trotsky, *The History of the Russian Revolution* (London, 1977), p17.

42. Noam Chomsky, *Necessary Illusions* (London, 1989), pviii.

43. http://www.isj.org.uk/index.php4?id=722&issue=130

44. http://www.youtube.com/watch?v=ZTONyRPId-U

45. http://www.isj.org.uk/index.php4?id=722&issue=130

46. Peter Robinson, "Portugal 1974-75: Popular Power", in Colin Barker (ed), *Revolutionary Rehearsals* (London, 1987), p83.

47. Tony Cliff, "Portugal at the Crossroads", in Tony Cliff, *International Struggle and the Marxist Tradition* (London, 2001), p235. http://www.marxists.org/archive/cliff/works/1975/portugal/3-masses.htm

48. Cliff, as above, p237.

49. Antonio Gramsci, *Selections from the Prison Notebooks* (London, 1971), p170.

50. Gramsci, as above, p129.

51. Karl Marx, "The Civil War in France", in *The First International and After* (London, 1974), p206.

52. Karl Marx, "The Civil War in France", as above, p209.